GETTYSBURG
The Confederate High Tide

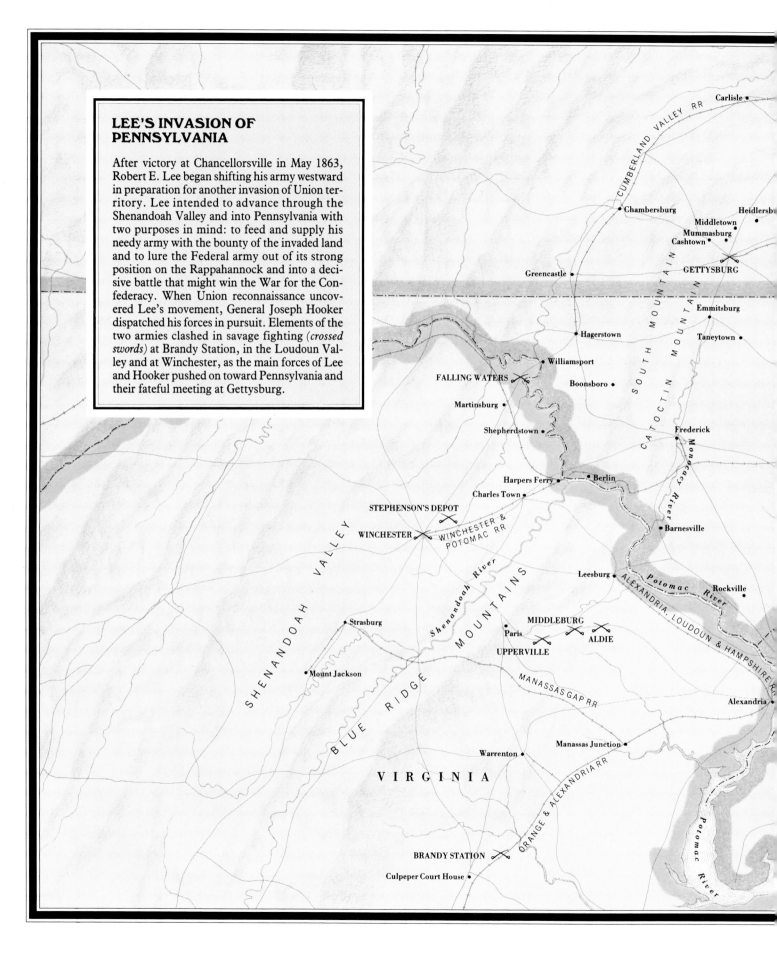

LEE'S INVASION OF PENNSYLVANIA

After victory at Chancellorsville in May 1863, Robert E. Lee began shifting his army westward in preparation for another invasion of Union territory. Lee intended to advance through the Shenandoah Valley and into Pennsylvania with two purposes in mind: to feed and supply his needy army with the bounty of the invaded land and to lure the Federal army out of its strong position on the Rappahannock and into a decisive battle that might win the War for the Confederacy. When Union reconnaissance uncovered Lee's movement, General Joseph Hooker dispatched his forces in pursuit. Elements of the two armies clashed in savage fighting (*crossed swords*) at Brandy Station, in the Loudoun Valley and at Winchester, as the main forces of Lee and Hooker pushed on toward Pennsylvania and their fateful meeting at Gettysburg.

Carlisle

CUMBERLAND VALLEY RR

Chambersburg
Heidlersb
Middletown
Mummasburg
Cashtown
GETTYSBURG

Greencastle

Emmitsburg

Hagerstown
Taneytown

Williamsport
FALLING WATERS
Boonsboro

SOUTH MOUNTAIN

CATOCTIN MOUNTAIN

Martinsburg

Shepherdstown
Frederick

Monocacy River

Harpers Ferry
Berlin
Charles Town

STEPHENSON'S DEPOT
Barnesville

WINCHESTER
WINCHESTER & POTOMAC RR

SHENANDOAH VALLEY

Leesburg
Rockville

ALEXANDRIA, LOUDOUN & HAMPSHIRE RR

Potomac River

Strasburg
MIDDLEBURG
Paris
ALDIE
UPPERVILLE

Shenandoah River

BLUE RIDGE MOUNTAINS

Mount Jackson

MANASSAS GAP RR

Alexandria

Warrenton
Manassas Junction

V I R G I N I A

ORANGE & ALEXANDRIA RR

Potomac River

BRANDY STATION
Culpeper Court House

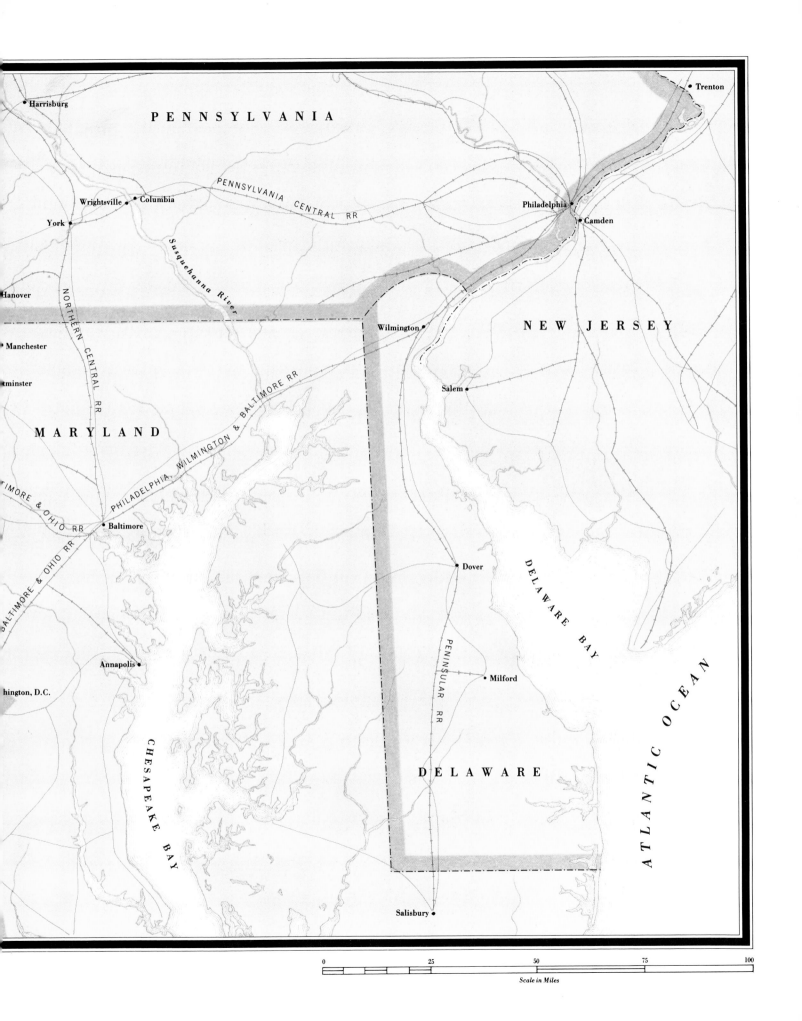

PENNSYLVANIA

• Harrisburg

Wrightsville • Columbia

York •

Hanover

• Manchester

minster

MARYLAND

TIMORE & OHIO RR

• Baltimore

BALTIMORE & OHIO RR

• Annapolis

hington, D.C.

CHESAPEAKE
BAY

PENNSYLVANIA CENTRAL RR

Susquehanna River

NORTHERN CENTRAL RR

PHILADELPHIA, WILMINGTON & BALTIMORE RR

Philadelphia

• Camden

Wilmington •

• Salem

• Dover

PENINSULAR RR

• Milford

DELAWARE

• Salisbury

• Trenton

NEW JERSEY

DELAWARE BAY

ATLANTIC OCEAN

0   25   50   75   100

Scale in Miles

THE
CIVIL
WAR

GETTYSBURG

BY

CHAMP CLARK

AND THE

EDITORS OF TIME-LIFE BOOKS

The Confederate High Tide

BARNES
&NOBLE
BOOKS
NEW YORK

1997 Barnes & Noble Books

ISBN 0-76070-646-6

Printed and bound in the United States of America

97 98 99 00 01 M 9 8 7 6 5 4 3 2 1

RDW

Gettysburg: The Confederate High Tide was originally published as part of the series:

The Civil War
Series Director: Henry Woodhead
Designer: Herbert H. Quarmby
Series Administrator: Philip Brandt George

Editorial Staff for *Gettysburg*
Associate Editors: Thomas A. Lewis (text); Jeremy Ross (pictures)
Staff Writers: Thomas H. Flaherty Jr., R. W. Murphy, David S. Thomson
Researchers: Kristin Baker, Brian C. Pohanka (principals); Harris J. Andrews
Copy Coordinators: Kelly Banks, Stephen G. Hyslop, Anthony K. Pordes
Picture Coordinator: Betty H. Weatherley
Editorial Assistant: Donna Fountain
Special Contributors: Brian McGinn, Leslie Marshall

Editorial Operations
Copy Room: Diane Ullius
Editorial Operations: Caroline A. Boubin (manager)
Production: Celia Beattie
Quality Control: James J. Cox (director)
Library: Louise D. Forstall

Correspondents: Elisabeth Kraemer-Singh (Bonn); Dorothy Bacon (London); Miriam Hsia (New York); Maria Vincenza Aloisi, Josephine du Brusle (Paris); Ann Natanson (Rome). Valuable assistance was also provided by: Carolyn Chubet (New York).

The Author:
Champ Clark, a veteran of 23 years as a correspondent, writer and senior editor for *Time*, retired from weekly journalism in 1972 in order to freelance and teach in the English Department at the University of Virginia. He is the author of numerous Time-Life Books, including *The Badlands* in the American Wilderness series, *Flood* in the Planet Earth series and *Decoying the Yanks* in the Civil War series.

The Consultants:
Colonel John R. Elting, USA (Ret.), a former Associate Professor at West Point, is the author of *Battles for Scandinavia* in the Time-Life Books World War II series and of *The Battle of Bunker's Hill, The Battles of Saratoga, Military History and Atlas of the Napoleonic Wars* and *American Army Life*. Co-author of *A Dictionary of Soldier Talk*, he is also editor of the three volumes of *Military Uniforms in America, 1755-1867*, and associate editor of *The West Point Atlas of American Wars*.

William A. Frassanito, a Civil War historian and lecturer specializing in photograph analysis, is the author of two award-winning studies, *Gettysburg: A Journey in Time* and *Antietam: The Photographic Legacy of America's Bloodiest Day*, and a companion volume, *Grant and Lee, The Virginia Campaigns*. He has also served as chief consultant to the photographic history series *The Image of War*.

Les Jensen, Director of the Second Armored Division Museum, Fort Hood, Texas, specializes in Civil War artifacts and is a conservator of historic flags. He is a contributor to *The Image of War* series, consultant for numerous Civil War publications and museums, and a member of the Company of Military Historians. He was formerly Curator of the U.S. Army Transportation Museum at Fort Eustis, Virginia, and before that Curator of the Museum of the Confederacy in Richmond, Virginia.

Michael McAfee specializes in military uniforms and has been Curator of Uniforms and History at the West Point Museum since 1970. A fellow of the Company of Military Historians, he coedited with Colonel Elting *Long Endure: The Civil War Years*, and he collaborated with Frederick Todd on *American Military Equipage*. He is the author of *Artillery of the American Revolution, 1775-1783*, and has written numerous articles for *Military Images Magazine*.

James P. Shenton, Professor of History at Columbia University, is a specialist in 19th Century American political and social history, with particular emphasis on the Civil War period. He is the author of *Robert John Walker* and *Reconstruction South*.

CONTENTS

General Hancock (*foreground*), commander of the Federal II Corps, orders his men to stem a Confederate advance at the climax of the Battle of Gettysburg.

A Hard Road North

"The warlike scene was fascinatingly grand beyond description. The battlefield presented a scenic view that the loftiest thought of my mind is far too low and insignificant to delineate, describe, or portray."

CORPORAL GEORGE M. NEESE, STUART'S HORSE ARTILLERY, ON THE BATTLE OF BRANDY STATION

On the clear, crisp morning of June 8, 1863, about a month after his victory at Chancellorsville, General Robert E. Lee arrived in the vicinity of Brandy Station, a whistle stop on the Orange & Alexandria Railroad a few miles north of Culpeper, Virginia, where most of his army was concentrating. There Lee was greeted by his chief of cavalry, Major General James Ewell Brown (Jeb) Stuart, resplendent in a brand-new uniform topped by a long, black ostrich plume fastened to his slouch hat with a golden clasp. He sat astride a horse bedecked with garlands of flowers. As the amused Lee later wrote to his wife, "Stuart was in all his glory."

Stuart had reason for pride: His command — now five brigades comprising 9,536 officers and men — had repeatedly demonstrated its ability to ride rings around the Federal cavalry. This day Stuart would put his superb force on display for Lee.

The horsemen were arrayed in double ranks on a plain just west of the Rappahannock River. Lee rode the three-mile line at a brisk trot. During his inspection he quietly noted some deficient carbines and saddlesore horses, and ordered corrective action. Then, his inspection complete, Lee took up station on a nearby hillock.

In response to a signal from Stuart, bugles blared, and the 22 cavalry regiments wheeled into a column of fours. With horses prancing to the airs of three bands, the troopers moved out beneath rippling flags. As Stuart led the parade past the admiring Lee, an immense cloud of dust arose from the churned-up ground.

The dust cloud was seen by a large Federal force — three cavalry divisions supported by two infantry brigades — that was at that moment descending on the Rappahannock from the east, bent on destroying Stuart's corps.

The mission had been ordered by the commander of the Army of the Potomac, General Joseph Hooker, whose intelligence service had reported Stuart's recent move from Fredericksburg to the Culpeper area. Fearing that Lee planned to strike northward, Hooker decided to take preemptive action, and he directed his cavalry commander, Brigadier General Alfred Pleasonton, to "disperse and destroy the rebel force."

As evening approached and Stuart's troopers were walking their horses back to their encampments after the grand review, Pleasonton's command of about 11,000 men moved silently into the woods on the opposite side of the river. At dawn they would attack, launching the largest cavalry engagement ever fought on American soil.

This battle would be the opening clash of a campaign that would come to climax at a small Pennsylvania town named Gettysburg. To that community of about 2,000 inhabitants, the armies of the Union and the Confederacy would be inexorably drawn in long and toilsome marches, as if by a directing destiny. And there, on 25 square miles of surrounding countryside, 160,000 Americans would fight in a terrible battle for which

While commanding at Gettysburg, the usually dour General George G. Meade was, an aide said, "quick, bold, cheerful and hopeful."

Lieutenant Colonel Joseph Dickinson, wearing a straw hat, and other members of General Joseph Hooker's staff relax near Fairfax Court House during the hiatus after the Battle of Chancellorsville. Perusing a book with Dickinson is Count Ferdinand von Zeppelin, an observer from the Prussian Army. Standing is Captain Ulric Dahlgren, who would lose a leg in the Gettysburg Campaign.

neither commander was prepared. Begun almost by accident, the struggle took on a life of its own, for three desperate days rising uncontrolled and uncontrollable to a crescendo of explosive violence. Gettysburg was Robert E. Lee's desperate gamble, his bid to win the climactic victory that would carry the War for the Confederacy. But when a deathly silence finally fell upon the blood-soaked battleground, Lee's cause had passed its highest tide, and the recession of Confederate hopes had begun.

The campaign that would lead to Gettysburg was dictated by the logic of Confederate circumstances. For all the glory of Lee's brilliant victory at Chancellorsville, he well knew that he had achieved little more than a postponement of the day when the the Army of the Potomac would again press his outnumbered and undersupplied army back toward Richmond. The problem of what to do next, Lee later explained, "resolved itself into a choice of one of two things: either to retire to Richmond and stand a siege, which must ultimately have ended in surrender, or to invade Pennsylvania."

The considerations that in September of 1862 had prompted Lee's march into Maryland — a drive that was blocked at Antietam — remained valid nine months later. A successful invasion might encourage Northern Peace Democrats in their agitation to end the War under terms reasonably favorable to the Confederacy; it might also induce British and French intervention on behalf of the Confederacy.

A more immediate impetus was provided

by the chronic shortage of supplies in the South. Hampered by an inadequate and inefficient railroad system, and operating in a war-ravaged region partly occupied by the enemy, Lee was unable to provide adequate food and clothing for his army or forage for its horses. As he told Major General Henry Heth, "The question of food for this army gives me more trouble and uneasiness than anything else." An invasion of Pennsylvania would provide his soldiers access to the rich farmlands of that state and allow the people of Virginia time to stockpile supplies.

On May 14, eight days after Hooker's withdrawal from Chancellorsville north across the Rappahannock, Lee had traveled to Richmond to confer with President Jefferson Davis and the Confederate Cabinet. The atmosphere was one of deepening melancholy: Stonewall Jackson had just been laid to rest in a Lexington graveyard; there was a tenuous stalemate in the East; and in the West, the Federals under General Ulysses S. Grant were relentlessly maneuvering toward Vicksburg.

For three days, Lee argued his invasion plan before a fretful audience. Jefferson Davis was uneasy about the idea, and Postmaster General John Reagan, a blunt Texan whose concerns lay west of the Mississippi, strenuously insisted that Lee instead send troops to the relief of Vicksburg. Yet such

General Alfred Pleasonton (right), chief of the revitalized Federal cavalry, poses with a dapper, ringletted George A. Custer. Pleasonton was so impressed with Custer's ability and dash that he jumped him in rank from captain to brigadier general.

In early June 1863 John Sedgwick's Federal reconnaissance force pauses on the west bank of the Rappahannock south of Fredericksburg after crossing the pontoon bridges in the background. The presence of A. P. Hill's Confederate corps, left behind to mask the westward movement of the rest of Robert E. Lee's army, convinced Sedgwick that Lee's entire force remained in the area.

was the power of Lee's magisterial presence that the group eventually approved his proposal by a vote of five to one.

Before setting out on the march north, however, Lee reorganized his army, using the sad imperative of replacing Stonewall Jackson to make some long-needed changes. The Army of Northern Virginia had been organized in two corps, one under Jackson and the other commanded by Lieutenant General James Longstreet. Each corps comprised about 30,000 men — too many, Lee thought now, for one officer to handle. Lee decided to divide his army into three corps.

The Confederate I Corps would remain under the command of Longstreet, the solid Georgian whom Lee fondly called "my old warhorse." In fact, Longstreet found the risks involved in Lee's invasion plan appalling. But, he wrote later, he agreed to the campaign, "provided it should be offensive in strategy but defensive in tactics, forcing the Federal army to give us battle when we were in strong position and ready to receive him." Longstreet believed that Lee had accepted that stipulation, and felt betrayed by subsequent events.

The selection of Lieutenant General Richard S. Ewell to take Jackson's place as head of II Corps was no surprise. Ewell had served doughtily under Jackson in the Shenandoah Valley and elsewhere, had lost a leg in the Second Bull Run Campaign and had been absent from the Army for nine months. Now he was ready to fight again.

To lead the new III Corps, Lee chose a man whom he praised as "the best soldier of his grade with me." Lieutenant General Ambrose Powell Hill was indeed a fierce fighter. Yet he was also high-strung and impatient, and more than once he had gotten in trouble

by attacking without waiting for orders. How he would respond to higher responsibility remained to be seen.

Lee also strengthened Stuart's cavalry by placing under his command four cavalry brigades that had been operating independently — including that of Brigadier General William E. Jones, whose quarrelsome, complaining ways had earned him the nickname of "Grumble." In stark contrast to the gaudy, gregarious Stuart, Jones wore blue jeans and a homespun jacket. Stuart and Jones detested each other, and the ill will between them would soon boil over.

Lee announced his appointments on May 30. Four days later, his infantry began moving up the Rappahannock toward Culpeper, first stop on the way north.

Across the river, meanwhile, the sorely perplexed commander of the Union's Army of the Potomac pondered his situation. After Chancellorsville, Major General Joseph Hooker had quickly recovered some of his old bluster, insisting in a letter to President Lincoln that "no general battle was fought at Chancellorsville." That being the case, Hooker concluded, "we lost no honor at Chancellorsville."

But Hooker had destroyed his credibility, not only with the government, as would soon become apparent, but with his own army as well. His senior corps commander, Major General Darius N. Couch, had been so outraged at Hooker's vacillating conduct during the battle that he refused to serve any longer under "Fighting Joe." Couch was transferred to command of the Department of the Susquehanna, with headquarters at Harrisburg, Pennsylvania, and was replaced at the head of II Corps by Major General Winfield Scott Hancock.

At least two other corps commanders, Major Generals Henry W. Slocum and John Sedgwick, were maneuvering to have Hooker replaced. But Abraham Lincoln, who had had little luck with his command changes in the Army of the Potomac, seemed in no hurry to make another. He told a visiting general that he was "not disposed to throw away a gun because it missed fire once."

On May 27, Hooker's intelligence chief had reported that "the Confederate army is under marching orders" and would probably "move forward upon or above our right flank." On June 4, Hooker learned from observers in balloons that some of the enemy's camps around Fredericksburg had been abandoned. Hooker proposed to Washington that he cross the Rappahannock and "pitch into" the troops Lee had left behind.

The President wasted no time in scotching that notion. Within an hour, he wired Hooker that any such move against an entrenched enemy, with another Confederate force of unknown size possibly operating north of the Rappahannock, could result in the army's being "entangled upon the river, like an ox jumped half over a fence and liable to be torn by dogs front and rear, without a fair chance to gore one way or kick the other."

Baffled and frustrated, Hooker sought more information, and a few days later he learned that Confederate cavalry had concentrated in the Culpeper area. It was then that Hooker dispatched Brigadier General Alfred Pleasonton's Cavalry Corps toward Brandy Station.

Forbidden to light fires, the Federal troopers on the banks of the Rappahannock on June 8 ate a cold supper, then slept with the reins of their still-bridled horses looped around their wrists. Four miles northeast of Brandy Station, at Beverly Ford, Brigadier General John Buford was preparing to lead the attack of the right wing — three brigades of cavalry supported by one of infantry. More than five miles downstream, southeast of Brandy Station, an even larger Federal force — a division under Brigadier General David McMurtrie Gregg and another commanded by French-born Colonel Alfred Duffié — was moving into position at Kelly's Ford.

According to Pleasonton's plan, Buford would make a frontal assault on the Confederate camps north of Brandy Station, while Duffié, and then Gregg, swung around and struck the enemy's right flank and rear. But as it neared time to attack, Duffié's men got lost in the darkness, and Gregg delayed his crossing of the river to wait for them. Thus, from the start, Pleasonton's carefully synchronized attack was thrown out of kilter.

On the other side of the Rappahannock, most of Stuart's men were blissfully unaware of the wrath about to descend on them. A single company of the 6th Virginia Cavalry patrolled the riverbank near Beverly Ford, while the rest enjoyed, in the words of an enlisted man, a "last sweet snooze."

At daylight General Buford's leading brigade, consisting of three regiments under Colonel Benjamin Franklin (Grimes) Davis, hero of the September 1862 siege of Harpers Ferry, splashed across the Rappahannock and swiftly broke through the thin Confederate picket line. Spearheaded by the 8th New York Cavalry, the Federal horsemen galloped hard, four abreast, down the narrow country road to Brandy Station.

Roused from their sleep, the Confederates hastened to mount up. Twenty-two-year-old Major Cabell E. Flournoy of the 6th Virginia

A Prussian Giant for the Confederacy

One of the more spirited Confederate counterattacks during the Brandy Station battle was led, as a Northern journalist put it, by a "giant, mounted on a tremendous horse, and brandishing wildly over his head a sword as long and big as a fence rail."

This apparition was no figment of the reporter's imagination but a bona fide member of Jeb Stuart's staff named Johann August Heinrich Heros von Borcke (*right*). Born in Prussia and an officer in the 2nd Brandenburg Dragoons, the six-foot-four-inch, 240-pound von Borcke set sail for America to seek adventure — and to evade his creditors at home — shortly after the Civil War began. He soon attached himself to Stuart's entourage as a volunteer aide. Promoted to major for his "fearless and untiring" service, von Borcke fought with his outsized, German-made Solingen sword (*below*) in most of the Virginia cavalry battles and skirmishes until, 10 days after Brandy Station, a neck wound received at Middleburg

Emulating his idolized leader, Jeb Stuart, Heros von Borcke wore a flowing mustache and a plume in his cavalry hat. He was 27 years old when he joined the Confederate Army on the eve of the Seven Days' Battles.

After the War, von Borcke and a fellow Prussian officer, Justus Scheibert — who was also present at Brandy Station — wrote an account of the battle in their native German.

Von Borcke's Huge Sword and Scabbard

put him out of action for the rest of the War.

Fierce in a fight, von Borcke was a mountain of amiability between battles. He amused his fellow officers by frequently recounting — and shamelessly embellishing — his martial exploits in his richly German-flavored English. He also proved adept at organizing dances and charades, and often starred in his own productions, dancing with elephantine grace while dressed in a woman's gown or, in a spoof of the Virginia state seal, lying on the floor in the role of Tyranny while a comely girl rested her foot on his neck. He also whipped up punches and eggnogs when the teetotaling Stuart was not looking.

Back in Germany after the War, a recovered von Borcke served with distinction in the Prussian Army. His passion for the Confederate cause and his adopted state never wavered, however. He flew the Confederate flag over his estate for the rest of his life, and he named his only daughter Virginia.

A mounted von Borcke warns Jeb Stuart, who is pulling on his boots, of the attack on Brandy Station.

gathered about 100 men and charged head-long at the oncoming Federals. Badly out-matched, Flournoy soon withdrew — but only after gaining some precious time for the Confederates.

Left behind by Flournoy's retreating Confederates was Lieutenant R. O. Allen, whose horse had been slightly wounded. Taking cover in a grove of trees, Allen spotted a Federal officer advancing in front of an enemy column. Allen decided to use the only bullet left in his revolver, at the closest possible range. He spurred his injured mount on.

The Federal officer, Colonel Davis, was looking back toward his men, waving them on with his saber. Sensing Allen's attack at the last instant, Davis turned and slashed wildly with his saber. But the Confederate avoided the cut by swinging to the side of his horse — and at the same time, he fired his last bullet. As Allen galloped to safety, Grimes Davis fell dead, shot through the brain.

Jeb Stuart had heard the deadly rattle of small-arms fire while he was drinking his morning coffee in his headquarters tent next to the red-brick Barbour House. The house was situated on Fleetwood Hill, a long and commanding north-south ridge that rose about a half mile northeast of Brandy Station. Stuart's supply train was loaded and ready to accompany the cavalry on its move north, scheduled to begin that morning. While his staff was scurrying about, hastily dressing and saddling the horses, an alarmed Stuart dispatched the wagons rearward to safety in Culpeper. Then he issued orders for reinforcements to move toward the fighting near Beverly Ford.

As Buford's Federals advanced farther, they came up against Brigadier General Wade Hampton's brigade, formed in line of

A lover of music and dancing, the chief of Confederate cavalry, Major General James Ewell Brown (Jeb) Stuart, carried his own minstrels with him. Always present, on the march and in bivouac, was a banjo player named Sam Sweeney; for dances, two fiddlers joined Sweeney along with a slave called Mulatto Sam, who played the bones and danced an inspired buck and wing.

battle at the edge of a wood near Saint James's Church. Major Robert Morris, a Philadelphia blue blood who commanded the 6th Pennsylvania Cavalry, was ordered to clear the enemy from his front. Morris deployed his men and charged.

"We flew along — our men yelling like demons," recalled Captain Henry Whelan of the 6th. "Grape and canister were poured into our left flank and a storm of rifle bullets on our front. We had to leap three wide, deep ditches, and many of our horses and men piled up in a writhing mass in those ditches and were ridden over." The charge faltered, and the Confederates counterattacked, capturing Major Morris and driving his troopers back in savage hand-to-hand fighting.

Buford's troopers began to fall back toward the Rappahannock. As they did so

Cavalrymen battle with sabers over a prized trophy, a regimental flag, in an artist's depiction of the sort of close combat waged at Brandy Station. A trooper of the 1st New Jersey Cavalry recalled that one guidon changed hands six times during the battle, ending up back with the Federals.

groups of cavalrymen dismounted to form skirmish lines alongside infantrymen who had come up in support. Just as the Confederate regiments were gathering for a decisive charge, Grumble Jones received bad news from his scouts: A column of dust had been seen rising from the direction of Kelly's Ford. Jones instantly sent word to Stuart that Federals had crossed the river downstream. Stuart was incredulous — and issued a scornful reply: "Tell General Jones to attend to the Yankees in his front, and I'll watch the flanks." Jones accepted the rebuff with grim humor, remarking: "So he thinks they ain't coming, does he? Well, let him alone, he'll damned soon see for himself."

Indeed, the Federal flanking force under Duffié and Gregg had found its bearings and was coming on fast. At a crossroads three miles beyond Kelly's Ford, the force split: Duffié continued westward toward Stevensburg, a village about five miles south of Brandy Station, to menace the Confederate rear; Gregg's column turned north on a road heading straight for Brandy Station. The way was wide open for Gregg — and Fleetwood Hill, which commanded his approach, was virtually undefended.

Hurrying off toward the fight near Beverly Ford with three brigades, Stuart had left behind at Fleetwood Hill only his adjutant, Major Henry McClellan, and a few couriers. McClellan did not believe a report he received that Gregg had outflanked the Confederates, but went to look for himself. "And so it was!" he wrote later. "Within cannon shot of the hill a long column of the enemy filled the road, which here skirted the woods. They were pressing steadily forward upon the railroad station, which would in a few moments be in their possession."

By chance, a single howitzer was near the foot of Fleetwood Hill, having been withdrawn from the battle near the river when ammunition ran low. It was only a 6-pounder, but it would have to do. Without an instant to spare, McClellan ordered the gun's commander, Lieutenant John W. Carter, to move the piece to the crest of the hill and commence firing. Scrounging in his limber box, Carter found some round shot and a few shells, and was soon lobbing them toward the oncoming enemy.

In the vanguard of the Federal troopers was a brigade of three regiments under the command of Colonel Sir Percy Wyndham, a veteran British soldier of fortune. Uncertain of the enemy strength, Wyndham halted

The 2nd United States Cavalry, part of John Buford's division, gallops forward between two retiring Federal units *(left and right)* in one of the last charges of the day at Brandy Station. Buford's troopers were repulsed by W.H.F. "Rooney" Lee's Confederate brigade, supported by artillery firing from Fleetwood Hill *(background, left)*.

to wait for the rest of Gregg's division.

McClellan, meanwhile, had sent a courier galloping to warn Stuart of the threat, but this was not Stuart's day for accepting reality. "Ride back there and find out what all this foolishness is about," he ordered a staff officer. Just then another courier rode up to confirm the news — and any remaining doubt was dispelled by the sound of Carter's howitzer opening up on Fleetwood Hill.

Stuart acted fast, dispatching four more artillery pieces to Fleetwood Hill and pulling two of Grumble Jones's regiments out of the line and sending them rearward up the ridge as fast as they could ride. They neared the crest just as Carter, his pitiful supply of ammunition completely gone, was with-

drawing. The Federal horsemen were now approaching at the gallop. "Not fifty yards below," Major McClellan recalled, "Colonel Percy Wyndham was advancing the 1st New Jersey Cavalry in magnificent order, in column of squadrons, with flags and guidons flying."

Without pausing, Jones's troopers galloped over the crest and down the far slope, headlong into Wyndham's charging horsemen. The opposing ranks met with what one trooper remembered as a "dead, heavy crash," and it was the Confederates who gave ground. "They broke like a wave on the bow of a ship," recalled Adjutant Marcus Kitchen of the 1st New Jersey, "and over and through them we rode, sabering as we went." Kitchen saw his regimental commander, Lieutenant Colonel Virgil Broderick, gallop into a squad of Confederates, running one man through with his saber, slashing another across the forehead and shooting a third before he was ridden down by a dozen Confederates.

Kitchen was riding to his commander's assistance when two Confederates set upon him. "The first one fired at me and missed," Kitchen later wrote. "Before he could again cock his revolver, my saber took him in the neck. The blood gushed out in a black looking stream; he gave a horrible yell and fell over the side of his horse." The adjutant went full tilt at the second Confederate, but his horse was shot from under him and he was hurled to the ground, where he lay semi-conscious while the fight raged around him.

Wyndham had taken a bullet in the leg, but he led his men on up the slope, overrunning the four Confederate artillery pieces. Some artillerists fought back with revolvers, while others wielding handspikes and spongestaffs knocked Federal troopers from the saddle. Just as the Federal momentum ebbed, fresh Confederate units entered the fray, driving Wyndham's scattered regiments back down the hill.

At the foot of the slope, the men of the 6th New York Battery had just unlimbered three guns when the 35th Virginia Battalion under Lieutenant Colonel E. V. White galloped into them. "The men at the battery fought with desperation," White reported. "There was no demand for a surrender or offer of one until nearly all the men were either killed or wounded." Caught up in the melee, a Federal trooper noticed "one Rebel, on a splendid horse, who sabered three gunners while I was chasing him. He wheeled in and out, would dart away, and then come sweeping back and cut down another man in a manner that seemed almost supernatural." Of the 36 New York artillerists, only six escaped death, wounds or capture.

With the tide of battle turning against him, General Gregg sent an urgent appeal to Colonel Duffié to ride immediately to the sound of the guns. To the northeast, meanwhile, Buford was again trying to force the Confederate position near Saint James's Church. Again the 6th Pennsylvania charged, only to be met and repulsed by the 9th Virginia. As batteries of horse artillery fired over their heads, the 2nd U.S. Cavalry, tough Regular Army troops, galloped into the fray. "There was little halting to make prisoners," noted Captain Wesley Merritt of the 2nd U.S. "Those who surrendered were told by a motion to go to the rear, and those who resisted were sabered or shot till they reeled from their saddles, the victor rushing madly on to engage a new foe."

Yet the Regulars were unable to effect the breakthrough, and eventually they were pushed back by the 2nd North Carolina and 10th Virginia. The battle around the church was winding down now; one of the last Confederate casualties there was Robert E. Lee's 26-year-old son, Brigadier General W.H.F. (Rooney) Lee, who was shot in the thigh as he led his brigade in a final charge.

Off to the southeast, Duffié had hooked around to Brandy Station from Stevensburg, but he arrived too late to present any real threat. In the end, General Stuart and his Confederates held Fleetwood Hill. At 4:30 p.m., Pleasonton began pulling his men back across the Rappahannock in good order. The Federals had suffered 866 men killed, wounded or missing compared with 523 Confederate casualties. But the creditable performance of Pleasonton's troopers against the legendary Stuart had given them a new sense of confidence that would sustain them through the balance of the War. The Battle of Brandy Station, wrote Henry McClellan, *"made* the Federal Cavalry."

The fighting at Brandy Station required Stuart to rest and refit his battered regiments, thereby delaying his northward movement by a full week. But Lee was not waiting for anyone, and on the afternoon of June 10, the day following the cavalry clash, he put Ewell's II Corps on the road. With the crippled Ewell traveling in a buggy, the corps crossed the Blue Ridge at Chester Gap, and by June 13 the divisions of Major Generals Edward Johnson and Jubal A. Early were moving into position near Winchester. That crossroads and rail terminus of 3,500 inhabitants in the northern Shenandoah Valley lay directly athwart the Confederate invasion route, and Lee did not intend to leave its garrison of 5,100 Federals behind him as he marched to the north.

For the past week, Union General in Chief Henry W. Halleck had been trying to get his commander at Winchester, Major General Robert H. Milroy, to move from that exposed position to the relative safety of Harpers Ferry, 30 miles to the northeast. But Milroy had insisted that he could hold Winchester "against any force the Rebels could afford to bring against it."

On June 13, Early's vanguard attacked outlying Federal detachments south of Winchester. After a sharp skirmish, Milroy ordered his men to withdraw to three forts

Major General Robert Milroy blamed General Hooker and the Federal cavalry for the disaster suffered by his command at Winchester. He should have been warned, he said, that the Confederate army was approaching: "I deemed it impossible that Lee's army with its immense artillery and baggage trains could have escaped from the Army of the Potomac."

north and west of the town. The next day President Lincoln wired Milroy's department commander, Major General Robert C. Schenck: "Get Milroy from Winchester to Harpers Ferry if possible. If he remains he will get gobbled up, if he is not already past salvation."

It was too late. That very morning at dawn, Ewell had seen that the key to Winchester lay in the three forts. A long, wooded ridge offered cover to within a thousand yards of the westernmost fort, which dominated the other two. Ewell ordered part of Early's division to advance through the woods and launch an assault on the fort. Meanwhile, Brigadier General John B. Gordon's brigade of Early's division would demonstrate against Milroy from the south, and Johnson's division would threaten Winchester from the east.

Early's movements took time, but they went undetected — even by General Milroy. Belatedly concerned about his situation, the Federal commander had himself hoisted in a basket to the top of a flagpole in the West Fort. "All day," wrote a Union staff officer, "under a burning sun, did General Milroy keep his position in lookout, and with a glass anxiously scan for sign of the enemy; but none was manifest."

Shortly after 5 p.m. the Confederates suddenly emerged from the woods, unlimbered 20 guns and opened fire on the West Fort. Federal artillery responded, steadily at first but with gradually diminishing effect as the fort's guns fell victim to the relentless Confederate bombardment. At about 6:30, there came the keening of the Rebel yell as Brigadier General Harry T. Hays's Louisiana Brigade descended headlong on the West Fort.

From his command post to the south, a

wildly excited Ewell cheered on the assaulting force. "Hurrah for the Louisiana boys!" he cried. "There's Early! I hope the old fellow won't be hurt!" At that instant Ewell was struck in the chest by a spent Minié ball. He was badly bruised, but the injury did not dampen his enthusiasm. Moments later, as darkness fell, Hays's men took possession of the West Fort and turned their guns on the routed defenders.

At about 10 o'clock that night, General Milroy, thinking himself surrounded, ordered an evacuation to Harpers Ferry. But Ewell, correctly predicting Milroy's reaction, already had ordered Johnson's division to march across country to intercept the fleeing Federals.

At about 3:30 a.m., Johnson arrived at a bridge that spanned a deep railroad cut near Stephenson's Depot, four miles northeast of Winchester on the turnpike to Harpers Ferry. Riding forward with his staff to reconnoiter, Johnson heard the sound of voices, the nickering of horses and the clop of hoofs on the turnpike: It was Milroy's force.

After a brief exchange of shots between advance scouts, and before Johnson could organize an assault, the Federals attacked. With his 6,000 men, Milroy vastly outnumbered Johnson, who had only 3,500 on hand. Another Confederate brigade, under Brigadier General James Walker, was still an hour away. But Milroy squandered his advantage by attacking piecemeal.

The brunt of Milroy's successive attacks fell on the Confederate brigade commanded by Brigadier General George H. (Maryland) Steuart, so nicknamed for his devotion to his native state. Steuart quickly positioned his men in the shelter of the railroad cut, and he ordered a gun from Captain William De-

Lieutenant Randolph McKim, a University of Virginia student and relative of Robert E. Lee, became a hero of the Stephenson's Depot battle when he rode forward to man a dangerously exposed Confederate artillery piece. In the thick of the fighting later at Gettysburg, the intrepid McKim was hit by shell fragments four times but survived the battle — and the War — to become a clergyman in Washington, D.C.

ment's battery rolled out onto the narrow bridge. Soon the ground in front of the railroad cut was strewn with dead and wounded Federals. Yet Milroy would not give up, and again the blue ranks came on. Thirteen of 16 Confederate gunners fell around their cannon on the bridge, but the gun still blazed away, served by a handful of staff officers and infantry volunteers. One of the officers, Lieutenant Randolph McKim, later wrote, "At every discharge, the recoil carried the gun almost over the side of the bridge, but before it could roll over, brave men were at the wheel, rolling it back into its place. We served the Federals with grape and canister. They were within 20 yards."

The battle raged through the night. Milroy's troops charged repeatedly until the Confederates were nearly out of ammunition. And then, with the first gray streaks of dawn, Walker's Confederates came out of the south and threw themselves into the fight. The battle was nearly over. The 13th Pennsylvania Cavalry staged a valiant last charge, but its ranks were shattered by Confederate artillery fire; 300 of the 600 troopers went down. The Federal formations broke, and men fled in all directions, great numbers of them falling into the hands of the enemy. Ewell's victory was sweet. At Winchester and at Stephenson's Depot, the Confederate II Corps had inflicted 443 casualties and captured 3,358 prisoners, 23 guns and 300 wagons, at a cost of only 269 casualties. Ewell had passed his first test as a corps commander in grand style.

On June 15, as Ewell's corps was still rounding up prisoners, Lee ordered his other two commanders — Longstreet at Culpeper and A. P. Hill at Fredericksburg — to move up in a hurry. Laboring beneath a scorching sun, more than 500 of Longstreet's men dropped out of the first day's march, some of them dying by the roadway. One soldier recalled the ordeal: "men crowding you at each elbow, stepping on you from behind, and getting in your way in front, stirring up a tornado of dust and making one's eyes ache."

Longstreet's troops crossed the Blue Ridge through Ashby's and Snicker's Gaps on June 19 and entered the Shenandoah Valley. Longstreet intended to turn north toward the Potomac, but Lee ordered him back into the mountain passes. Jeb Stuart, who had moved north from Brandy Station on June 16, was having trouble preventing the Federal cavalry from breaking through his screen east of the Blue Ridge. Longstreet would have to help plug the mountain gaps until A. P. Hill, who was following the route previously taken by Ewell, could make his way through the Shenandoah Valley.

Stuart had left Brandy Station in a resentful mood; criticism of his handling of the battle there had been severe. Accurately insisting that Stuart and his generals had been caught by surprise, the Richmond *Examiner* blamed it on "vain and empty-headed officers." Intoned the Richmond *Sentinel:* "Vigilance, vigilance, more vigilance, is the lesson taught us by the Brandy surprise. Let all learn it, from the Major General down to the picket." Presciently, Hooker's chief of staff, Major General Daniel Butterfield, warned Washington that such public criticism would doubtless require Stuart "to do something to retrieve his reputation."

But for the present, Stuart had to content himself with the hard, thankless job of preventing Pleasonton's cavalry from learning what the Confederate infantry was doing west of the Blue Ridge. Between June 17 and 21 a series of vicious little cavalry skirmishes erupted on the Loudoun Valley roads leading westward to the Blue Ridge gaps (*pages 27-29*). Pleasonton pushed Stuart back as far as Ashby's Gap in the Blue Ridge but could go no farther. His troopers were exhausted, and his horses breaking down.

Stuart had cause for satisfaction in having prevented the enemy from penetrating his screen. But he had grander ideas, and he soon put them before Lee at the commander's headquarters in the village of Paris.

Lee had wanted the cavalry to accompany the infantry into Pennsylvania. But Stuart urged that he be allowed to harass Hooker, delaying the Federal army's pursuit. Lee agreed, but he stipulated that as soon as Hooker crossed the Potomac, Stuart must take position on the right flank of the Confederate infantry. Keenly aware of Stuart's propensity for the dramatic, Lee put his admonition in writing on June 22; and on the 23rd, after Stuart had suggested crossing the river east of Hooker to get between the Federal army and Washington, Lee sent still another order — among the War's most fateful.

Specifically, the document addressed itself to Stuart's options "if General Hooker's army remains inactive" south of the Potomac. In that case — and, presumably, only in that case — Stuart was told that he "would be able to judge whether you can pass around their army without hindrance, doing all the damage you can, and cross the river east of the mountains. In either case, after crossing the river, you must move on and feel the right of Ewell's troops."

When the order reached Stuart near Middleburg late on the rainy night of June 23, he scarcely noticed that the letter's discretionary clause depended on Hooker's continuing inertia. Stuart gleefully read it as permission to embark on an adventure that promised to make up for his embarrassment at Brandy Station.

Early the next morning he issued his orders. His two largest brigades — those of Beverly Robertson and Grumble Jones, with a total of about 3,000 men — would remain behind to guard the Blue Ridge passes, then protect the Confederate supply line as the infantry passed through Maryland on the way to Pennsylvania. But the three best brigades — Wade Hampton's, Fitzhugh Lee's and Rooney Lee's (commanded by Colonel John R. Chambliss while Rooney Lee recovered from his wound received at Brandy Station) — would assemble at Salem and prepare to move on. Around 1 a.m. on June 25, Stuart's column trotted out of Salem, heading east. For the next eight days, so far as Lee was concerned, his cavalry chief — upon whom he relied for information about enemy movements — might just as well have been on another planet.

Meanwhile, the long, undulating gray lines moved north from Winchester, with Ewell's divisions under Johnson, Early and Major General Robert Rodes crossing the Potomac near Shepherdstown between June 15 and 18. Spirits were high, especially among the soldiers from Maryland. When General George (Maryland) Steuart reached the far bank, he leaped from his horse, kissed the ground and stood on his head in joy.

On June 19, Ewell sent his lead division under Rodes on up the Cumberland Valley toward Chambersburg, 20 miles beyond the Maryland-Pennsylvania border. On June 22, Lee ordered Ewell to advance along a broad front, letting his "progress and directions" be shaped by the "development of circumstances." If the Pennsylvania capital of Harrisburg "comes within your means," Lee added, "capture it."

Two days later Rodes entered Chambersburg. Johnson's division was following, and Early's was pushing north on a parallel road 10 miles to the east. That same day, Hill's and Longstreet's corps began crossing the Potomac at Shepherdstown and Williamsport. The Confederates were moving fast; one soldier wrote that in a single day he had savored "breakfast in Virginia, whiskey in Maryland, and supper in Pennsylvania."

On June 25, Ewell organized the next phase of his advance. He would accompany Rodes and two of Johnson's brigades as they drove northeast through Carlisle to Harrisburg. Johnson's third brigade would head west to forage, while Early's division would march eastward to York and from there to Wrightsville, a town on the Susquehanna. This route would take him through the prosperous farming center of Gettysburg.

Early was off at daybreak the next morn-

Clash of Sabers in Loudoun Valley

In the clash at Aldie, Major Henry Lee Higginson of the 1st Massachusetts (*above*) was sabered, shot and left for dead. He survived and after the War met Colonel Thomas Rosser of the 5th Virginia Cavalry (*left*), who had inflicted the saber cut on the Major's right cheek.

In the third week of June 1863, some of the most savage mounted actions of the War unfolded on the rolling pastures of Virginia's Loudoun County, east of the Blue Ridge.

Ordered by General Hooker to scout Lee's army, General Alfred Pleasonton sent columns of Federal horsemen toward the Blue Ridge gaps and the Shenandoah Valley beyond. En route, they encountered Jeb Stuart's cavalry screen. The fighting began at 4 p.m. on June 17 when General Judson Kilpatrick's brigade ran into Colonel Thomas Munford's Confederates astride the Little River Turnpike near the village of Aldie.

The impetuous Kilpatrick committed his regiments piecemeal and nearly met with disaster. Firing from the crest of a haystack-crowned ridge, a dismounted squadron of the 5th Virginia Cavalry blunted charge after charge. When Kilpatrick sent the 1st Massachusetts galloping in a flank attack, the regi-

At Aldie, Captain George Custer spurs ahead of the 1st Maine as Colonel Calvin Douty falls dead (*left*) and General Judson Kilpatrick is unhorsed.

Firing their Sharps carbines, dismounted troopers of the 1st Maine advance during the battle at Middleburg. So close were the opposing lines that one officer reported, "We could look our foemen in the eye."

ment was ambushed in a narrow sunken road and lost nearly half of its men. Colonel Munford reported, "I have never seen as many Yankees killed in the same space of ground." It was 7 p.m. before the outnumbered Confederate cavalrymen withdrew.

Kilpatrick was supposed to rendezvous that day with Colonel Alfred Duffié's 1st Rhode Island at Middleburg, five miles west of Aldie. But Kilpatrick failed to do so, and when Duffié arrived at Middleburg, he was surrounded by three Confederate brigades. Not until early morning on June 18 was Duffié able to cut his way out of the trap; he had lost 214 of his 300 men.

On June 19, Stuart's men withdrew to a ridge west of Middleburg and met the attack of General David Gregg's Federal division. All day long dismounted skirmishers blazed away as horse-artillery shells shrieked overhead. In late afternoon Stuart fell back to the next ridge, and Gregg called off the pursuit.

The following day a driving rainstorm halted operations, but on June 21 the fighting flared up again. Deploying a brigade of infantry detached from V Corps and using his artillery to advantage, Pleasonton pushed Stuart eight miles west to Upperville, at the foot of the Blue Ridge. There Stuart turned and stood in an attempt to cover his line of retreat through Ashby's Gap.

East of the town, Gregg's division was checked by General Wade Hampton's Confederates in a saber-swinging melee, while a mile north of town Union General John Buford's charging troopers, slowed by stone walls and ditches, were halted by General William "Grumble" Jones's men. The Federals soon renewed their attacks, however, forcing Stuart back through Upperville. As his regiment thundered down the village streets, a soldier of the 1st Maine recalled, "it seemed that I heard but the gallop of one mighty horse." At 6 p.m. Stuart retreated into Ashby's Gap, covered by an infantry brigade posted at the summit. Content to rest on his laurels, Pleasonton went into camp for the night. In five days of fighting, 613 Federal and 510 Confederate troopers had been killed, wounded or captured.

Pleasonton had failed to pinpoint Lee's army. Even so, the battles in the Loudoun Valley bolstered the confidence that the Federal cavalry had recently found at Brandy Station. "Around our flickering fires the bold troopers gave vent to many a yarn," one Federal soldier later recalled, "expressing their complete satisfaction at the defeat of Jeb Stuart's Confederate riders hitherto considered invincible."

As supporting artillery fires overhead, Federal cavalrymen charge through the orchards and fields west of Upperville in pursuit of Stuart's retreating forces.

Confederate prisoners stand under guard at Fairfax Court House, Virginia. They were among the 58 men of Captain Reuben Boston's squadron of the 5th Virginia Cavalry captured at Aldie.

ing. Grim, grizzled, stooped with arthritis, spewing tobacco juice and oaths with equal facility, he was not a commander from whom the enemy could expect tender treatment. Late on the afternoon of June 26, Early's division approached Gettysburg, which was defended by a regiment of raw Pennsylvania militia mustered into government service only four days previously. The militiamen had arrived in town the night before, and when they saw Early's veterans deploying against them, they did not linger long. "It was well that the regiment took to its heels so quickly," Early remarked sardonically, "or some of its members might have been hurt."

Gettysburg's civilians long remembered their first sight of Lee's famed foot soldiers. "Most of the men," recalled one Pennsylvanian, "were exceedingly dirty, some ragged, some without shoes, and some surrounded by the skeletons of what had once been an entire hat." Another observer was more respectful, noting that all were "well armed and under perfect discipline. They seemed to move like one vast machine."

Early demanded that the people of Gettysburg turn over to him the equivalent of $10,000 in goods and produce, but the town's merchants and farmers had already removed or hidden most of their commodities. Early, in a hurry to get on to York, took time for no more than a desultory search. But before he left he noticed that the town possessed a shoe factory, and he sent word back to A. P. Hill that Gettysburg might be a good place to get some badly needed shoes.

York, nearly 30 miles from Gettysburg, surrendered to Early's leading brigade on the evening of June 27. As the Confederate troops rode through town the next morning, they were in high spirits. Noting that the residents who lined the streets seemed in sullen humor, Brigadier General William (Extra Billy) Smith decided that they needed some cheering up. Smith, one of the Army's quainter characters, had won his nickname for wrangling extra payments while he was a civilian mail contractor. A former Virginia governor, his instincts ran more along political than military lines, and now, given a captive audience, he felt compelled to deliver what he called a "rattling, humorous speech" from the saddle.

"My friends," he began, "how do you like this way of coming back into the Union? I hope you like it; I have been in favor of it for a long while. We are not burning your houses or butchering your children. On the contrary, we are behaving ourselves like Christian gentlemen, which we are."

The speaker was just getting warmed up when his division commander came pushing through the crowd and seized him by the blouse. "General Smith!" shouted a furious Jubal Early. "What in the devil are you about, stopping the head of this column in this accursed town?" Replied Smith: "Having a little fun, General, which is good for all of us." Whereupon Extra Billy Smith, silenced but unchastened, cheerfully resumed his eastward march.

Another orator fared better. The gallant General John B. Gordon, seeing that many of the ladies in the crowd were frightened by the fierce appearance of his troops, paused to reassure them, saying "that the spirit of vengeance and rapine has no place in the bosoms of these dust-covered but knightly men." When he had concluded, a young girl ran out and thrust into his hand a bouquet of flowers — in which was hidden a note, in a woman's handwriting, describing the disposi-

Confederate infantrymen marching north to Pennsylvania ford a stream with shoes off and trousers rolled. Many units crossed half a dozen rivers and creeks during Lee's advance, employing what one officer mordantly termed "Confederate pontoons — that is, by wading straight through."

tions of the 1,400 Federal militia defending Wrightsville, Early's next destination.

Upon reaching Wrightsville later that day, Gordon found the information to be accurate in every respect. But before he could seize the long covered bridge that crossed the Susquehanna from Wrightsville to the town of Columbia, the enemy set it afire. Early was thereby frustrated in an impromptu plan to swing left from Columbia and assail Harrisburg from the southeast while Ewell, coming up from Carlisle, attacked the capital from the southwest. With the bridge gone, Early had little choice but to recall his corps to York and await instructions from Ewell.

When those orders came, they were hardly what Early expected. On June 27, Rodes's troops had entered Carlisle after an uneventful march from Chambersburg. Ewell had proudly raised the Confederate flag over the U.S. Army cavalry barracks where he had been stationed before the War, and he had sent a cavalry brigade under Brigadier General Albert Gallatin Jenkins on toward Harrisburg. On the night of June 28, Jenkins camped on a hill four miles from the Pennsylvania capital. It was the northernmost penetration made by any Confederate Army unit during the War.

After some sharp skirmishes with Federal

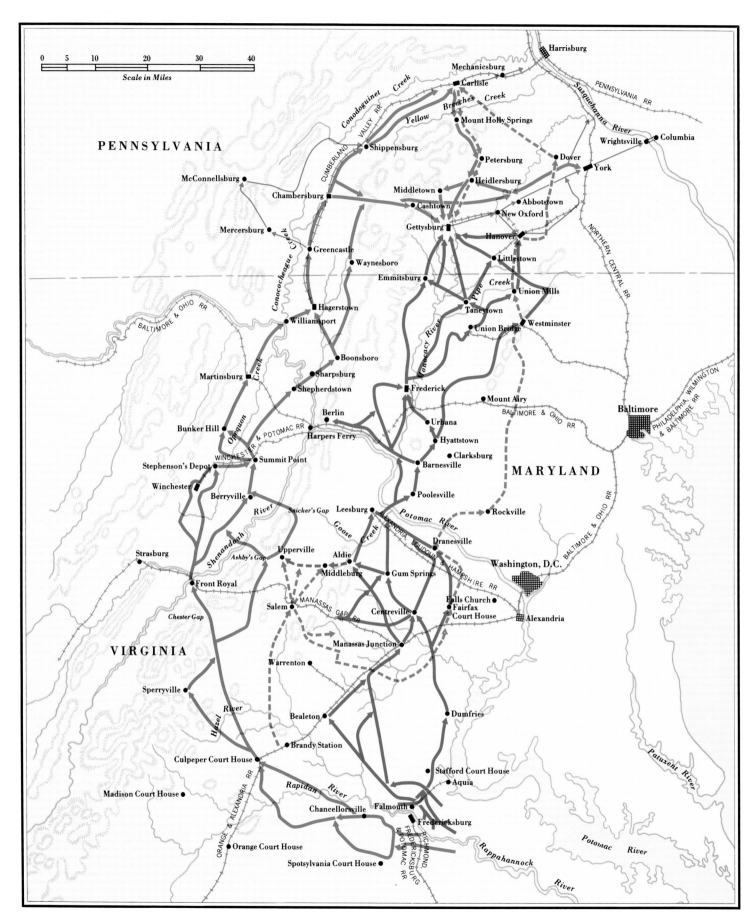

PENNSYLVANIA

McConnellsburg
Mercersburg
Greencastle
Waynesboro
Hagerstown
Williamsport
Boonsboro
Sharpsburg
Shepherdstown
Martinsburg
Bunker Hill
Stephenson's Depot
Winchester
Berryville
Summit Point
Harpers Ferry
Berlin
Strasburg
Front Royal
Upperville
Middleburg
Salem
Aldie
Sperryville
Bealeton
Brandy Station
Culpeper Court House
Madison Court House
Chancellorsville
Orange Court House
Spotsylvania Court House

Harrisburg
Mechanicsburg
Carlisle
Mount Holly Springs
Shippensburg
Chambersburg
Middletown
Cashtown
Gettysburg
Petersburg
Heidlersburg
New Oxford
Abbotstown
Hanover
Littlestown
Emmitsburg
Union Mills
Taneytown
Westminster
Union Bridge
Frederick
Mount Airy
Urbana
Hyattstown
Clarksburg
Barnesville
Poolesville
Rockville
Leesburg
Dranesville
Gum Springs
Centreville
Falls Church
Fairfax Court House
Alexandria
Manassas Junction
Warrenton
Dumfries
Stafford Court House
Aquia
Falmouth
Fredericksburg

Dover
York
Wrightsville
Columbia

Baltimore
Washington, D.C.

MARYLAND
VIRGINIA

32

On June 10, 1863, Robert E. Lee started his three corps northward toward Pennsylvania, with Richard Ewell in the lead, on a route (red line) through the Shenandoah Valley, across the Potomac and into the Cumberland Valley's rich farmlands. On June 13, Joseph Hooker began to move on a parallel march (blue line), shifting the Army of the Potomac from the Fredericksburg area to Manassas, then to Frederick, Maryland. After screening Lee's daring thrust for eight days, Jeb Stuart left Salem, Virginia, on June 25 with three cavalry brigades on a foray (broken red line) that took the horsemen entirely around the Federal army.

A letter home from Charles W. Reed, a Massachusetts artilleryman and later a well-known artist, includes a vivid sketch of weary Federal infantrymen slogging through northern Virginia behind a shot-up banner. Reed, whose battery followed these footsore troops north, won the Medal of Honor for gallantry at Gettysburg.

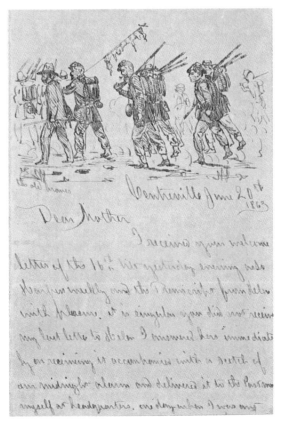

troops west of the Susquehanna, Jenkins reported that Harrisburg looked like easy pickings, and Ewell made plans for an attack. But then, on June 29, urgent word came from Lee. Ewell's entire corps was ordered to withdraw immediately and march south to Gettysburg. The Army of Northern Virginia was concentrating for battle.

Behind Lee's surprising order lay one of the War's stranger stories. Back in Virginia before the campaign had begun, Longstreet had sent a spy to Washington to learn what he could about the Army of the Potomac's movements. The agent was a slim, stooped man with a brown beard and hazel eyes, who went only by the name of Harrison.

On the night of June 28, Longstreet's chief of staff, Lieutenant Colonel G. Moxley Sorrel, was awakened, in his words, by "a detail of the provost guard bringing up a suspicious prisoner. It was Harrison, the scout, filthy and ragged, showing some rough work and exposure."

Taken to Lee, Harrison reported that he had learned that Hooker's army was moving north. In fact, he had followed it to Frederick, Maryland, where at least two Federal corps were already encamped.

Somehow procuring a horse and buggy, Harrison had hurried on to Chambersburg; on the way he had seen other Federal troops heading toward South Mountain, beyond which lay the Cumberland Valley and Lee's vital supply line.

"I have no confidence in any scout," Lee had said, and certainly the bedraggled Harrison was no sight to inspire trust. But with Stuart gone no one knew where, Lee had no other source of information, and Longstreet vouched for Harrison's reliability. Before the night was over, Lee accepted Harrison's report and ordered the army to concentrate in order to prevent the Federals "from advancing farther west, and intercepting our communications with Virginia."

Almost incidentally, Harrison remarked upon leaving Lee's presence that Hooker had been relieved of command and that the Army of the Potomac was now led by a little-known general named Meade.

Since mid-June Hooker had seemed in a fog. "He acts like a man without a plan," complained one of his staff officers, "and is entirely at a loss what to do, or how to match the enemy, or counteract his movements." Remarkably, Hooker himself seemed to agree, at one point writing to Halleck, "I don't know whether I am standing on my head or feet."

After Brandy Station, Hooker had begun to slide his army to the northwest, and by June 19 it was spread between Manassas and Leesburg, near the Potomac. There it remained for almost a week, until most of Lee's army had moved north through Maryland. Not until June 25, as Ewell was starting his march from Chambersburg to Carlisle, did the Federal army bestir itself to give chase. By the time it was across the river on June 27, Fighting Joe Hooker had only a few hours left as its commander.

In fact, Hooker's downfall had been ordained shortly after his retreat from Chancellorsville. President Lincoln, Secretary of War Edwin Stanton and General in Chief Halleck had agreed that Hooker's conduct there had been inexcusable and that he must not be allowed to lead the army in another major battle. But they also decided that to remove him immediately would have political repercussions they could not afford; they would wait until the explosive general tendered his resignation over some dispute, and they would accept it.

Hooker did not give them the opportunity until the next battle was dangerously near. But finally he became incensed by Halleck's refusal to permit the abandonment of Maryland Heights, overlooking Harpers Ferry, and the reassignment of the 10,000-man garrison there. On the afternoon of June 27, Hooker fired off a message from his headquarters at Frederick, Maryland, asking that he be relieved of command. No doubt he intended to prod the Administration into giving him what he wanted. Instead, he had given the Administration what it wanted.

By evening, Colonel James A. Hardie of the War Office staff was on a special train bound for Frederick. There, Hardie hired a horse and buggy, and drove several miles south of town to the V Corps encampments. At about 3 a.m. on June 28, he found the tent of the V Corps commander, Major General George Gordon Meade.

Unceremoniously awakened to receive his visitor, Meade thought at first that he was for some reason being arrested. When informed that he was instead being placed in command of the army, he tried to refuse, protesting that other generals — especially Major General John Reynolds — were both senior and better qualified. Finally, told that the assignment was an order, not a request, he gave in. "Well," he said, "I've been tried and condemned without a hearing, and I suppose I shall have to go to execution."

A graduate of West Point, Meade had served competently as an Army engineer in the Mexican War. In the present war, he had risen on a reputation of toughness and reliability to the rank of major general. His courage and skill at Fredericksburg had earned him a corps commander's appointment before the Battle of Chancellorsville. At the age of 47, he was less than compelling in appearance and personality. Tall, gaunt, bearded and balding, with wire-rimmed glasses that failed to conceal the dark pouches beneath his eyes, he was ordinarily of a quiet, bookish nature. Yet he was noted more than anything else for his hair-trigger temper. Colonel Theodore Lyman, a member of Meade's staff and a longtime friend, wrote: "I don't know of any thin old gentleman, with a hooked nose and cold blue eyes, who, when he is wrathy, exercises less of Christian charity than my well-beloved chief!"

Though he ranked last in the class of 1847 at West Point, Henry Heth later proved himself an able general, serving in Braxton Bragg's Confederate army in Tennessee before being transferred at Lee's request to the Army of Northern Virginia. Two months after receiving command of a division, he launched the attack that sparked the Battle of Gettysburg.

Without delay, Colonel Hardie escorted Meade to Hooker's headquarters to effect the change in command. Hooker accepted the hard news gracefully — and with apparent relief. As Meade later wrote to his wife, Hooker told him that "he was ready to turn over to me the Army of the Potomac; that he had enough of it, and almost wished he had never been born." When the uneasy session was over, Meade went to work.

The task was awesome. Hooker had left Meade with no plan at all — not even a precise idea of the army's disposition. Yet by late that afternoon Meade had determined that all the corps were within easy range of Frederick and developed a strategy. "I must move toward the Susquehanna," he wired to Halleck, "keeping Washington and Baltimore well covered, and if the enemy is checked in his attempt to cross the Susquehanna, or if he turns toward Baltimore, give him battle."

By evening Meade had issued orders for the troops to "be ready to march at daylight tomorrow." By nightfall the next day, June 29, the blue host had marched nearly 25 miles and was arrayed along a 20-mile front extending southeast from Emmitsburg, Maryland, near the Pennsylvania border, to Westminster.

On learning that A. P. Hill and Longstreet were camped east of Chambersburg on the road to Gettysburg, Meade strengthened the wing closer to the enemy by ordering Major General Daniel E. Sickles' III Corps to close on John Reynolds' I Corps and Major General Oliver O. Howard's XI Corps near Emmitsburg. John Buford's cavalry division, ranging ahead, entered Gettysburg at about 11 a.m. on June 30. The troopers found the townsfolk wildly excited about the sudden approach and withdrawal, just a few minutes before, of a Confederate infantry brigade.

That force — under Brigadier General James Johnston Pettigrew of Henry Heth's division in A. P. Hill's corps — had come looking for shoes. On nearing the town, Pettigrew had ridden ahead to reconnoiter. Pausing on a ridge, he swept his field glasses across the landscape. Gettysburg itself seemed empty of enemy troops — but then he saw a long column of Federal cavalry, coming fast up the road from Emmitsburg.

Since Pettigrew had been instructed to find shoes, not a fight, he withdrew to the west, halting his brigade nearly four miles from Gettysburg. That afternoon he rode back to Cashtown to tell Heth what he had seen. Just then, A. P. Hill came up and listened to the conversation. But he placed no stock in Pettigrew's story, insisting that "the enemy are still at Middleburg, and have not yet struck their tents." Henry Heth said: "If there is no objection, General, I will take my division tomorrow and get those shoes." Replied Hill: "None in the world."

That night at Gettysburg, John Buford listened quietly as one of his brigadiers opined that the Confederates, last seen heading the other way, would not return — and that if they did, he would easily beat them off. Despite his avuncular way, Buford was as tough and hardheaded a man as any in the Army, and he knew better. "No, you won't," he said. "They will attack you in the morning and they will come booming — skirmishers three deep. You will have to fight like the devil until supports arrive."

This silk guidon was carried by I Troop of the 6th Pennsylvania Cavalry. Guidons were used to show the location of mounted units in battle.

FREDERICKSBURG,

CHANCELLORSVILLE,

GETTYSBURG.

Soldiering on Horseback

The cavalry, so Civil War infantrymen often complained, led an easy life, galloping splendidly about the countryside instead of slogging wearily along on foot. But in fact the horse soldiers had to earn the privilege of riding into battle through hard work, long hours and the mastering of skills unknown to the average rifleman.

The cavalryman, first of all, had to know how to care for his mount, even to the extent of putting his horse's comfort ahead of his own. He had to learn to maneuver his horse through the bewildering evolutions required to move masses of cavalry. And on campaign, he was expected to fight both mounted and dismounted, to scout enemy positions, to intercept the enemy's cavalry, to protect the army's flanks, to carry dispatches, to scour the countryside for forage and even to act as a military policeman. "There is no rest for the cavalryman," one veteran Confederate horse soldier lamented. "He is ever in the saddle."

This homemade wool guidon was carried by a company of the 1st Maryland Cavalry. It is a small version of the 1861 Confederate national flag.

Lieutenant Thomas B. Dewees leads I Troop, 2nd U.S. Cavalry, in a column of twos near its camp at Falmouth, Virginia, in the summer of 1863.

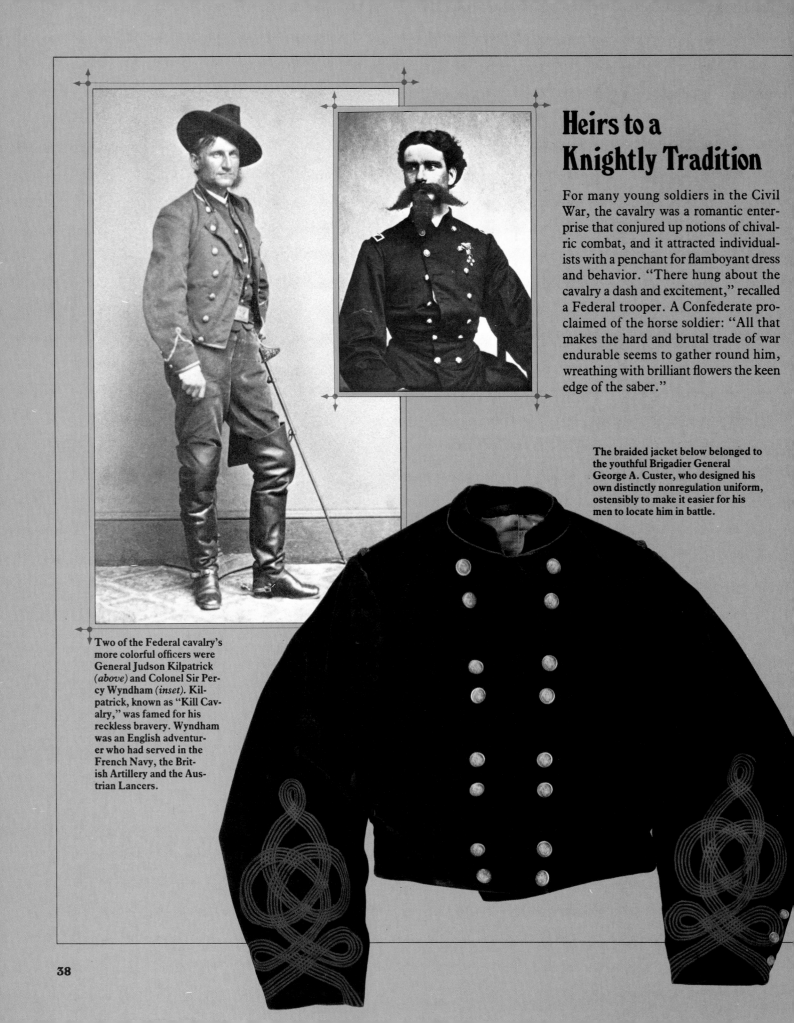

Heirs to a Knightly Tradition

For many young soldiers in the Civil War, the cavalry was a romantic enterprise that conjured up notions of chivalric combat, and it attracted individualists with a penchant for flamboyant dress and behavior. "There hung about the cavalry a dash and excitement," recalled a Federal trooper. A Confederate proclaimed of the horse soldier: "All that makes the hard and brutal trade of war endurable seems to gather round him, wreathing with brilliant flowers the keen edge of the saber."

The braided jacket below belonged to the youthful Brigadier General George A. Custer, who designed his own distinctly nonregulation uniform, ostensibly to make it easier for his men to locate him in battle.

Two of the Federal cavalry's more colorful officers were General Judson Kilpatrick (*above*) and Colonel Sir Percy Wyndham (*inset*). Kilpatrick, known as "Kill Cavalry," was famed for his reckless bravery. Wyndham was an English adventurer who had served in the French Navy, the British Artillery and the Austrian Lancers.

The rakish trooper shown at far left was one of many Confederate cavalrymen to adopt the jaunty style of their leader, Jeb Stuart. Others emulated the carefree manner of Stuart's favorite subordinate, the large and jovial Fitzhugh Lee (*inset*). Prince Jerome Bonaparte, visiting a Confederate cavalry camp, wrote: "Nothing is as picturesque as the southern cavalry; they wear the most impossible outfits."

These officer's gauntlets are embroidered with flowers and lined with morocco leather; plainer versions were issued to troopers to wear while riding.

Private James W. Poague of the 1st Virginia Cavalry ornamented the upturned brim of his hat with an elaborate leather star.

Fancy spurs, such as the gilt, eagle-headed version above, were popular with cavalry officers. A few spurs were even made in solid gold.

Arms and Equipment of a Cavalry Trooper

Armed with carbine, saber, and one or two pistols, the Civil War horse soldier took more than 20 pounds of equipment into battle. He wore the gear on his person so that the weapons would be handy if he had to dismount and fight on foot.

Most Federal cavalry units used breech-loading carbines of various sorts; more than 17 different types were issued during the War. Confederate troopers usually had to make do with muzzle-loading, smoothbore carbines — or even shotguns. Most horsemen on both sides continued to carry sabers, although firearms proved more effective in combat.

Both the jaunty, cigar-smoking Federal trooper (*lower left*) and his Confederate counterpart (*left*) wear full equipment over short shell jackets, which were common to enlisted cavalrymen on both sides. The jackets were far more convenient for riding than the longer, skirted frock coats.

Essential to a cavalryman was his belt, which carried his saber and revolver, a small box of percussion caps and a larger box for ammunition. The holster was of a cross-draw design and was usually worn on the right; this allowed the trooper to draw his revolver with his left hand while wielding the saber with his right.

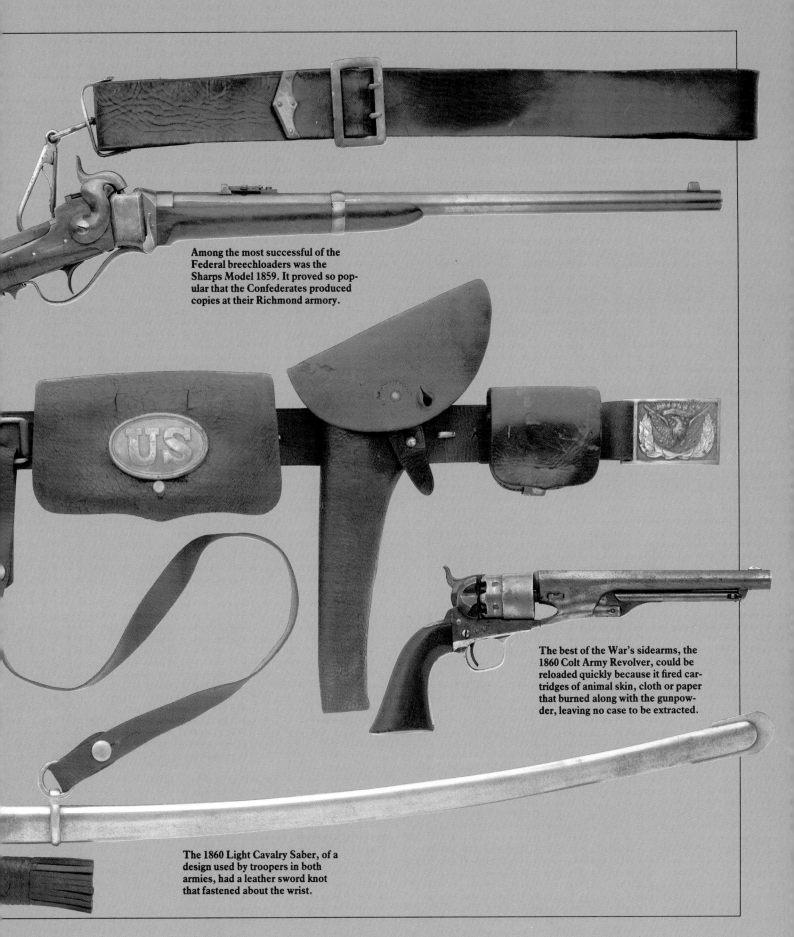

Among the most successful of the
Federal breechloaders was the
Sharps Model 1859. It proved so popular that the Confederates produced
copies at their Richmond armory.

The best of the War's sidearms, the
1860 Colt Army Revolver, could be
reloaded quickly because it fired cartridges of animal skin, cloth or paper
that burned along with the gunpow-
der, leaving no case to be extracted.

The 1860 Light Cavalry Saber, of a
design used by troopers in both
armies, had a leather sword knot
that fastened about the wrist.

The rugged McClellan saddle, designed by Union General George McClellan, was the best of several types used during the War. The trooper strapped his overcoat across the saddle bow and a poncho and blanket across the cantle. Saddle bags and other items were hung on straps.

Private Elnathan S. Cheney of the 2nd Pennsylvania Cavalry sits proudly astride his mount. Cheney's tack is a mixed bag: He has combined the standard McClellan saddle with a nonregulation bridle.

In bivouac, the 14-inch iron picket pin was driven into the ground and linked by rope to the horse's halter. This arrangement allowed the animal to graze without straying.

The Importance of Maintaining a Mount

The cavalry trooper was quick to learn that his ability to fight — perhaps even to survive — depended on his horse. Each man acted as his own groom and veterinarian and maintained his own tack. He made certain that saddle and bridle fit properly to keep his mount free of sores, sprains and even internal injuries. And he kept the horse well fed. Indeed, in the Confederate Army, where rations were often scarce, horses ate even when their riders did not.

This single-reined bridle with curb bit was of a pattern introduced in 1863. It replaced a more complicated double-reined model that used two bits, a snaffle and a curb; that rig was discarded after it proved too difficult for novice cavalrymen to control.

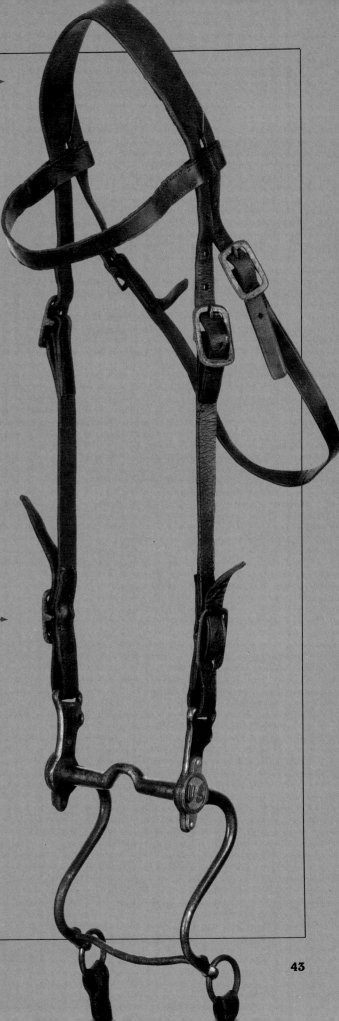

43

The Push to Seminary Ridge

"For a mile up and down the open fields before us the splendid lines of the veterans of the Army of Northern Virginia swept down upon us. Their bearing was magnificent. They came forward with a rush, and how our men did yell, 'Come on, Johnny, come on!'"

LIEUTENANT COLONEL RUFUS R. DAWES, 6TH WISCONSIN, THE IRON BRIGADE

2

The Confederate foragers appeared at first as ghostly shapes in the drizzly dawn of Wednesday, July 1, 1863. Lieutenant Marcellus E. Jones, in charge of pickets for the 8th Illinois Cavalry, saw them at about 5:30 a.m., marching in a shadowy column down the Chambersburg Pike from Cashtown, approaching the stone bridge across Marsh Creek three miles west of Gettysburg.

From his position on the pike 700 feet away, Jones saw a mounted Confederate officer pull off to one side to let the infantrymen pass. Borrowing a carbine from one of his sergeants, Jones fired at the enemy horseman without visible result, then prudently withdrew as the Confederates deployed a line of skirmishers a mile and a half wide.

Jones had fired the first shot in what would begin as a minor skirmish between a few Confederate infantry brigades looking for shoes and two Federal cavalry brigades keeping track of enemy movements. But from the moment that hasty shot was fired, events outraced strategy, feeding on capricious circumstance until 70,000 Confederates and 90,000 Federals were drawn into a monumental battle that would become etched in the national memory.

Neither army was ready to give battle on the 1st. General Lee, unfamiliar with the terrain and ignorant of the Federal strength in the area, insisted that no general engagement be started until his army was concentrated between Cashtown and Gettysburg; Ewell was several hours away to the north, and

Longstreet's corps almost a day's march to the west. As for the Federals, General Meade had directed his engineers to lay out a defensive line 20 miles southeast of Gettysburg along Pipe Creek, and earlier that morning he had told his corps commanders to be prepared to fall back to it. But the choice of a battlefield was already out of the generals' hands; a desperate struggle had begun in the ridges west of Gettysburg.

The ridges ran generally north-south. A mile and a half from the town, Major General Henry Heth's advancing Confederates first encountered Herr Ridge, named after a tavern on its crest. Nine hundred yards to the east, across a swale through which meandered a sluggish little stream called Willoughby Run, was McPherson's Ridge, where a farm family of that name lived. Adjoining their farm, a few hundred yards to the south of the Chambersburg Pike, stood the 17-acre patch of McPherson's Woods.

Another 500 yards to the east, about three quarters of a mile from Gettysburg, lay Seminary Ridge; crowned by the three-story brick Lutheran Theological Seminary, it rose gently 40 feet above the surrounding fields. A short distance north of the pike, Seminary Ridge merged with McPherson's Ridge; from there a single promontory, Oak Ridge, continued northward to an 80-foot-high knob named Oak Hill that dominated the area northwest of Gettysburg.

The pike, which traversed these ridges from the northwest, was paralleled about 200

Flag – 24th Mich. Vols. After Gettysburg.

yards to the north by a railbed, as deep as 20 feet in places, in which no track had yet been laid. Nine other roads radiated from Gettysburg to all points on the compass: Clockwise from the Chambersburg Pike these led to Mummasburg, Carlisle (to the north), Heidlersburg (and thence to Harrisburg), York, Hanover, Baltimore, Taneytown (to the south), Emmitsburg and Hagerstown.

When General Heth reached the crest of Herr Ridge at about 8 a.m., he saw that he would not get to McPherson's Ridge without a fight. Deploying his two leading brigades, Heth ordered them to move forward and occupy the town. North of the turnpike was a brigade commanded by Brigadier General Joseph R. Davis, a nephew of the Confederate President. Davis was untried in brigade command, and his four regiments had never

before fought together. South of the pike was a veteran brigade of Alabama and Tennessee troops under Brigadier General James J. Archer. A Princeton graduate, lawyer and veteran of the Regular Army, Archer had been warned the previous day by his fellow brigadier James Johnston Pettigrew that he might be heading for trouble. "Archer listened," wrote a member of Pettigrew's staff, "but believed not and marched on unprepared."

The Federal cavalry officer who had so accurately predicted this day's events, Brigadier General John Buford, was ready for Heth's advance. As Buford wrote later, "My arrangements were made for entertaining him." Buford placed the dismounted troopers of Colonel William Gamble's 1st Brigade along the east bank of Willoughby Run in a 1,000-yard line extending from the railbed south across the Chambersburg Pike. North of the railroad, Colonel Thomas Devin's 2nd Brigade reached to the base of Oak Hill. But the Federal line was woefully thin: Against Heth's 7,461 men, Buford counted only 2,748 troopers, with one in every four holding horses for his comrades. Buford knew he was outnumbered and sent urgently for reinforcements to Major General John F. Reynolds, commanding the Federal left wing.

As Heth's skirmishers came confidently down Herr Ridge toward Willoughby Run, their muskets gleaming beneath a sun now breaking through the overcast, they were staggered by a burst of fire from Gamble's men and salvos from Lieutenant John Calef's battery of horse artillery. Firing furiously with their breech-loading carbines, the Federals held up Heth's advance for a full hour. But by about 9 a.m. Buford could see from his observation post atop the Lutheran Seminary building that Gamble's troopers were being pushed back across Willoughby Run.

Just then General Reynolds rode up. "The devil's to pay!" exclaimed Buford. But when Reynolds asked if he could hold out a while longer, until reinforcements arrived, Buford replied simply: "I reckon I can."

That was good enough for Reynolds. "The enemy is advancing in strong force," he wrote to Meade at Taneytown. "I will fight him inch by inch, and if driven into the town I will barricade the streets and hold him back as long as possible." Still unsure about where to make his stand, Meade was nevertheless delighted with Reynold's firmness. "Good!" he exclaimed. "That is just like Reynolds, he will hold out to the bitter end."

Meade's high opinion of Reynolds was widely shared: A West Pointer, Reynolds was a crisply professional soldier who went about his business with very little fuss. At

Union cavalry general John Buford sits surrounded by his staff officers, whose performance in the Gettysburg Campaign, he wrote, "cannot be excelled in this army." Standing at the left is Captain Myles W. Keogh, a dashing Irish soldier of fortune who was Buford's favorite aide.

In the initial action at Gettysburg, dismounted troopers of Buford's cavalry division hold a defensive line against Confederate infantry at Willoughby Run. "My troops at this place had partial shelter behind a low stone fence, and were in short carbine range," wrote General Buford. "Their fire was perfectly terrific, causing the enemy to break."

42, he had been with the Army of the Potomac from the beginning and had repeatedly demonstrated that he could be relied upon. Moreover, he was a Pennsylvanian determined to rid his state of the Confederates.

He had decided the evening before to hold Gettysburg. Before riding off at dawn that day from his camp at Emmitsburg, 12 miles to the southwest, he had set his forces in motion: Brigadier General James A. Wadsworth was told to put his 1st Division of I Corps on the road to Gettysburg at once; Major General Abner Doubleday — in charge of I Corps while Reynolds served as overall commander of the Federal left wing — was assigned to bring up the rest of the corps. Reynolds also left orders for XI Corps to follow and recommended that III Corps move toward Gettysburg in support. Doubleday was slow to get his troops on the road — a

typical performance by a general who seldom did anything poorly enough to warrant criticism or well enough to attract applause.

About a mile short of Gettysburg, the men at the head of Wadsworth's column saw a rider approaching fast. It was Reynolds, returning from his meeting with Buford. He ordered the two leading brigades to advance across the fields directly toward the ridges west of town. Off they went, shucking their knapsacks and loading their muskets as they trotted toward McPherson's Ridge.

They reached the crest at about 10 a.m. and rushed into battle. Brigadier General Solomon Meredith's 1st Brigade — known as the Iron Brigade for its exploits at Groveton, South Mountain and Antietam — was on the left, extending through McPherson's Woods and on toward the south; the five regiments of Brigadier General Lysander Cutler's 2nd

Brigade were to Meredith's right, two just south of the Chambersburg Pike and three to the north. Gamble's hard-pressed cavalrymen, who were falling back to a reserve position, shouted encouragement as the soldiers moved through their ranks: "We have got them now. Go in and give them hell!"

Reynolds placed Captain James A. Hall's 2nd Maine Battery astride the turnpike and rode south to join the Iron Brigade in McPherson's Woods. As he turned in his saddle to urge on the 2nd Wisconsin, a skirmisher's Minié ball took him behind the right ear, and Reynolds fell dead from his horse. Doubleday, who had arrived on McPherson's Ridge only a few minutes before, was now the senior officer on the field.

South of the turnpike, meanwhile, the Confederates had advanced with little notion of what lay in store. The veteran brigade under James Archer crossed Willoughby Run and attacked recklessly through McPherson's Woods, the troops thinking they were up against only cavalry. But they soon saw, amid the smoke and flame in the woods, that their enemy wore the Iron Brigade's distinctive black felt hats, with wide brims turned up on the left side. "There are those damned black-hatted fellows again!" shouted one Confederate. "Tain't

A photograph taken from Seminary Ridge around July 15 shows the view of Gettysburg that confronted Confederate troops after they seized the ridge on July 1.

tanding in the cupola of the Luth-
ran Theological Seminary on Semi-
ary Ridge, Union Generals Buford
nd John Reynolds look toward the
ttacking Confederate columns of
eneral Henry Heth's division. The
ight convinced Reynolds that the
onfederates were present in force
nd that Gettysburg was the place to
tand and destroy Lee's army.

no militia. It's the Army of the Potomac!"

The Iron Brigade soon seized the advantage. The Federal line extended farther south than that of the Confederates, and in the brigade's advance the 19th Indiana and the 24th Michigan surged ahead, turned Archer's right flank and caught his men in a murderous enfilade. Unable to withstand such fire from both front and flank, Archer's Confederates made a hasty retreat back across Willoughby Run.

The Iron Brigade came after them, scooping up prisoners — among them Archer, who was collared by the burly Private Patrick Maloney of the 2nd Wisconsin. Archer was tak-

en to General Doubleday, a former comrade in the Regular Army, who greeted him with a certain lack of sensitivity. "Good morning, Archer," said Doubleday, "I am glad to see you." Replied Archer: "Well, I am *not* glad to see you by a damned sight."

All this while, on the Federal right north of the railroad grading, Cutler's 2nd Brigade had been furiously engaged. There, the tactical situation was reversed; Cutler's line was shorter than that of General Davis' Confederate brigade. Overlapping Cutler's right, the inexperienced 55th North Carolina wheeled with surprising precision to the

south and struck hard at the Federal flank and rear. From his position in Cutler's line, just north of the railbed, Captain J. V. Pierce of the 147th New York heard the dreaded cry: "They are flanking us on the right!"

With a disaster in the making, General Wadsworth was forced to order Cutler's three regiments north of the pike to pull back to Seminary Ridge. Two of them obeyed at once. But Lieutenant Colonel Francis C. Miller, commanding the 147th New York, fell with a bullet in his throat before he could repeat the order to withdraw. The New Yorkers, alone, unknowing and under assault from front and flank, fought on in a wheat field adjacent to the railbed before breaking for the rear.

Seeing the peril to their right, the red-trousered 14th Brooklyn and the 95th New York — the two Cutler regiments that had been posted south of the Chambersburg Pike — now faced to the north, marched to the road and began firing at the flank of Davis' Confederates as they ran in pursuit of Wadsworth's retreating regiments. The New Yorkers were soon joined by Doubleday's only reserve unit, the 6th Wisconsin of the Iron Brigade. The Wisconsin men rested their muskets on the fence bordering the pike and opened an enfilading fire into the 2nd Mississippi. The Confederates slowed, stopped, then broke for the only available cover — the banks of the railroad cut. Some of the Confederates milled around in the bottom of the 20-foot cut, others crawled up the side and started shooting.

From the protection of the cut, the Confederates were now able to pour a lethal fire into the ranks of the New York and Wisconsin men. As the Federals began to fall, Lieutenant Colonel Rufus Dawes of the 6th Wis-

consin ran to Major Edward Pye of the 95th New York. "We must charge!" Dawes cried. "Charge it is," replied Major Pye, and the two regiments headed across a field toward the cut, followed by the 14th Brooklyn. In the charge, 180 men of the 6th Wisconsin went down. But the Federals reached their objective, driving the Confederates from the rim of the cut in a brief, brutal exchange of gun butts and bayonets, and capturing the flag of the 2nd Mississippi. Soon the Confederates in the cut were surrounded and trapped. In the heat of battle, the Federal troops lining the rim could have conducted a frightful slaughter. Instead, a merciful impulse prevailed, and from the length of the Union line there arose a loud chorus: "Throw down your muskets. Down with your muskets."

So many Confederates surrendered that Colonel Dawes found himself encumbered by an "awkward bundle" of swords handed over by captured officers. Later, Federal soldiers found more than a thousand discarded Confederate muskets in the cut. General Davis had lost more than half of his 2,300 men, most of them as prisoners.

The remnants of Davis' command retired to Herr Ridge, joining Archer's shattered brigade there. As General Heth would later report, the enemy "had now been felt, and found to be in heavy force in and around Gettysburg."

At 11 a.m., an uneasy quiet fell over the battlefield, one that would last for more than two hours, punctuated occasionally by the sharp crack of muskets as skirmishers sniped at one another or by the deeper roar of cannon feeling at long range for enemy artillery positions. During the lull, the ridges and

Shot from the saddle at McPherson's Woods, General John Reynolds was among the most admired of Union officers — "one of the *soldier* generals," remarked an infantryman who served under him. He had purchased his Western style saddle while serving in the Mexican War. The sketch of him falling mortally wounded, by artist Alfred Waud, was probably based on eyewitness accounts

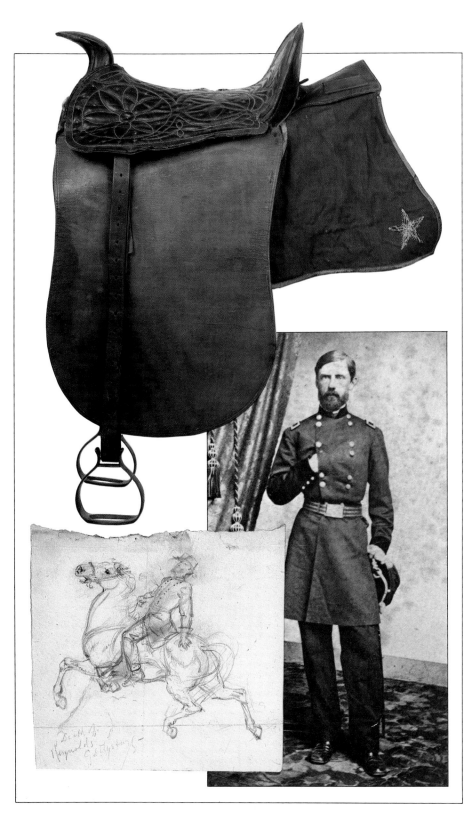

fields outside Gettysburg swarmed with soldiers moving from place to place in preparation for a renewal of the fighting; men in blue and in butternut marched for all they were worth in what had become a race between reinforcements.

Heth was still determined to occupy Gettysburg. He was encouraged by his corps commander, A. P. Hill, who, although ill that day and still back in Cashtown, sent word that Major General William Dorsey Pender was moving up to support Heth.

Meanwhile, the Federals readjusted their defenses. The Iron Brigade was recalled to its former line in McPherson's Woods and along the ridge to the south. Cutler's battered brigade moved the short distance from Seminary Ridge back to McPherson's Ridge north of the turnpike.

As these movements were being executed, a new commander — the fourth of the day — relieved Doubleday and took charge of the Federal forces on the battlefield. He was Major General Oliver O. Howard, who had arrived in Gettysburg in advance of his XI Corps at about 10:30 a.m. Howard had climbed to the top of one of the town's taller buildings just in time to see Cutler's men breaking for the rear.

Jumping to the wrong conclusion, Howard sent a courier galloping to Meade at Taneytown with what Abner Doubleday later described as "the baleful intelligence that the First Corps had fled from the field at the first contact with the enemy." A few minutes later, Howard was informed that Reynolds had been killed, and as the senior officer present he assumed command.

He was given little time to contemplate his new responsibilities. At about 12:30 p.m. there came the ominous news that a large body of Confederate infantry was approaching the exposed Federal right from the north. Moments later the Confederates ran 16 guns out of the woods onto Oak Hill and began firing at Cutler's line from a range of 800 yards. A Federal brigade under Brigadier General Henry Baxter was sent racing to deploy along Oak Ridge on Cutler's right.

These men were part of the veteran division commanded by Brigadier General John C. Robinson, an old Army Regular and a very tough customer — who looked the part. "In a much-bearded army," wrote a Federal officer, "he was the hairiest general I ever saw." Robinson placed Baxter's brigade behind a stone wall along a section of the Mummasburg road that faced generally north.

With only about 1,400 men, Baxter's brigade could hardly be expected to do more than briefly blunt a major enemy drive from the north. But just then, as luck would have it, the leading elements of Howard's own XI Corps came panting and sweating into Gettysburg on the run.

With commendable foresight, Howard left a division under Brigadier General Adolph von Steinwehr, along with some artillery units, on the commanding heights of Cemetery Hill, about a half mile south of the Gettysburg town square. "Boys," Howard told the troops, "I want you to hold this position at all hazards." Then Howard ordered Major General Carl Schurz, who had temporarily succeeded him in command of the corps, to rush the divisions of Brigadier Generals Alexander Schimmelfennig and Francis C. Barlow northward to meet the menace from that direction.

On the afternoon of July 1, Confederates of Colonel John Brockenbrough's Virginia brigade assault the Union defensive line extending from the McPherson farm into McPherson's Woods (*right*).

Since Schurz did not know where the Confederate infantry would attack, he had to cover all possibilities. The result was a thin, mile-long, east-west line that failed by a full quarter of a mile to hook up with the right flank of I Corps.

Scarcely had Schurz completed his deployment than out of the woods to his left appeared Confederates in battle line. They belonged to the 7,983-man division of Major General Robert Rodes, in Ewell's corps, and they clearly meant business.

In a rare bow to caution, A. P. Hill early that morning had notified Ewell, who was on the march from Carlisle, that Heth's division was on its way to Gettysburg, where Federal troops had been seen the day before. Ewell, in turn, had ordered the divisions of Rodes and Jubal Early to head directly for Gettysburg instead of the scheduled rendezvous with Lee near Cashtown. Later, Ewell received a message from Lee approving the change but warning that a general engagement was not to be brought on till the rest of the army came up.

Rodes and his troops approached Gettysburg from the northeast along the Heidlersburg road, followed at some distance by Early's division. About two miles from the town, Rodes turned west, toward the Mummasburg Road and Oak Hill. There, stretching away to the south along Oak Ridge, Rodes saw the right flank of the I Corps line — Cutler's brigade — and realized that it was wide open to assault from the north. As far as he could see, Rodes said later, the enemy "had no troops facing me at all."

Rodes, a lean 34-year-old with a tawny mustache and hard blue eyes, was an aggressive commander; the opportunity before him seemed far too good to pass up, despite Lee's warning against a general engagement. Rodes decided to attack. To preoccupy the Federals while his infantry was deploying, he summoned his artillery battalion under Lieutenant Colonel Thomas H. Carter and posted it on Oak Hill, where its flanking fire startled the exposed Federal line — and drew the quick response of General Robinson.

By the time Rodes had deployed his five brigades, the situation had changed. The men of Baxter's brigade were scurrying into their blocking position astride Oak Ridge, and the men of XI Corps were hurrying out of Gettysburg onto the plain east of the ridge; Rodes's advantage was rapidly evaporating. Shortly after 2 p.m., without further reconnaissance, without even bothering to throw out a line of skirmishers, Rodes attacked.

Rodes's haste soon exacted a heavy penalty. On his left was a brigade of Georgians led by Brigadier General George Doles; the men were veterans, and the quiet 33-year-old Doles was a fine officer. Moreover, he was directly in front of the inviting quarter-mile gap between the Federal XI Corps and Robinson, on the I Corps right. But Doles's brigade was held out of the initial assault, partly to contain the XI Corps and partly to provide a link with Early's division, expected to arrive from the northeast momentarily.

To Doles's right was a brigade of Alabamians under Colonel Edward A. O'Neal, who had performed clumsily at Chancellorsville. Beyond O'Neal was the North Carolina brigade of Brigadier General Alfred Iverson Jr., whose advancement in the Army was widely considered to be the result of family influence. In support on Iverson's right rear was a large brigade under Brigadier General Junius Daniel, a West Pointer who had just come to Lee's army from the North Carolina coast with an excellent reputation. And held in reserve was the small but formidable brigade of Brigadier General Stephen Dodson Ramseur, who at the age of 26 was already known as one of the Army's hardest fighters.

Rodes's dispositions placed the heaviest burden on O'Neal and Iverson, his two weakest commanders — and the whole affair was botched from the beginning. Iverson's brigade, which was supposed to attack abreast of O'Neal's, delayed to allow more time for the Confederate batteries on Oak Hill to clear the way. O'Neal's brigade therefore went forward alone — using only three of its five regiments.

Attacking on a narrow front down the eastern slope of Oak Ridge, the brigade ran fullface into a storm of musket fire from behind the stone wall along the Mummasburg road where Baxter's brigade had only minutes before taken its position. Soon 696 of O'Neal's 1,688 men were casualties. As Rodes later described it, with considerable understatement, "The whole brigade was repulsed quickly and with loss." And Rodes was enraged to find that Colonel O'Neal had chosen to remain with a reserve regiment rather than go into battle with his men. Neither did Iverson accompany his men when they belatedly began to move. Instead, he perfunctorily told his troops to "give them hell." With those words, as one of the embittered North Carolinians later wrote, Iverson's part "in the heroic struggle of his brigade seems to have begun and ended."

The collapse of O'Neal's attack left Iverson's left flank wide open, and so as the brigade moved down the western slope of Oak Ridge it began drifting toward the left. In its path was another stone wall that ran due south from the Mummasburg road. There, the Federals awaited: Immediately after sending O'Neal's regiments reeling back, Baxter had changed front, and his men now crouched hidden behind the wall Iverson's troops were approaching.

"Unwarned, unled as a brigade, we went to our doom," recalled Sergeant H. C. Wall of the 23rd North Carolina. "Deep and long must the desolate homes and orphan children of North Carolina rue the rashness of that hour."

Baxter and his men waited until the nearest Confederates were less than 80 yards away. Then they arose and delivered a volley that scythed down the Carolinians. More than 500 of the attackers fell in what a Confederate officer later described as a "line as straight as a dress parade." The Confeder-

Although he retained Lee's confidence, Major General Robert Rodes did not perform at Gettysburg with the skill that had won him a reputation at the Battle of Chancellorsville. Rodes's hasty and poorly coordinated attack on Oak Ridge cost his division 2,500 men.

As Heth's Confederates attack for the second time along the Chambersburg Pike near McPherson's barn (*background*), Color Sergeant Benjamin Crippen of the 143rd Pennsylvania shakes his fist at the enemy. Crippen's valor rallied his regiment, but it cost him his life.

ate formation, wrote Captain Isaac Hall of Baxter's 97th New York, "staggered, halted, and was swept back as by an irresistible current." Baxter's men now counterattacked, taking nearly 400 prisoners and destroying Iverson's brigade. The 23rd North Carolina alone lost 236 men, including all but one of its officers.

Watching the carnage from his position of relative safety, General Iverson became completely undone, hysterically reporting to Rodes that an entire regiment had changed its allegiance and gone over to the enemy. What Iverson had seen was a few of the survivors pitifully waving their handkerchiefs in surrender amid the ranks of the dead. Iverson had sent 1,384 men into a fight that lasted 15 minutes; no more than 400 were present when the brigade was finally reassembled. Iverson was so distraught that one of his staff officers, Captain D. P. Halsey, had to assume command and tend to what was left of the brigade.

As Iverson's few survivors were making their way to the rear, Daniel and Ramseur launched their brigades into the battle. Daniel took his 2,162 men to the right, southward down McPherson's Ridge, beyond the effective range of Robinson's and Cutler's infantry on his left. Daniel's aim was to get

Overrun by Confederates on McPherson's Ridge, several Federals of the 149th Pennsylvania fight with their fists to retrieve the captured colors carried by the Con-

federate at right. In the middle distance, Doubleday's Federal troops make a stand as the Confederates attack down the Chambersburg Pike toward Gettysburg.

onto the Chambersburg Pike, then push down the road to strike Cutler's left flank. It was a good idea, but Daniel was entirely unaware of the railroad cut that lay in his way.

Awaiting Daniel on the other side of the cut was the 149th Pennsylvania, one of three regiments in Colonel Roy Stone's Bucktail Brigade, whose men wore deer tails on their caps. The 149th, commanded by Lieutenant Colonel Walton Dwight, leveled a savage volley as Daniel's brigade approached. The stunned Confederates fell back, and the Bucktails charged through the railroad cut.

But as they closed on the Confederates, the Bucktails were enfiladed by A. P. Hill's guns to the west and forced to fall back to the cut. There, with smoke swirling about them, they waited until Daniel's advancing men were a mere 20 paces away, then delivered another murderous volley. Daniel's troops fell back only to come on again. The fight seesawed back and forth. Colonel Stone went down, severely wounded; so did his successor; so did Walton Dwight. In all, the Bucktail Brigade lost two thirds of its men before the day ended. But they held Daniel

Under heavy shelling, 19-year-old Lieutenant Bayard Wilkeson directs the fire of the four guns of Battery G, 4th U.S. Artillery, ranged along Barlow's Knoll on the Federal right. He and 17 others would become casualties in the fighting there. Wilkeson's father, *New York Times* correspondent Samuel Wilkeson, was at Meade's headquarters; he responded to news of his son's death by asserting bitterly that the position was one "where a battery should never have been sent."

Hit by a shell that nearly severed his right leg, Lieutenant Wilkeson coolly lay on a blanket, twisted his sash into a tourniquet and amputated the limb with the initialed pocket knife shown here. Hours later he died.

was forced to give ground foot by foot in the face of overwhelming pressure. The 16th Maine remained as a rear guard — at terrible cost, with 232 of its 298 men either killed, wounded or missing. As the Confederates closed in from all sides, the men tore their regimental flag to shreds rather than let it fall into enemy hands.

On Herr Ridge, a gray-bearded general on a gray horse was watching the spectacle. Robert E. Lee had arrived on the battlefield.

Lee had been cheerful that morning when he set out toward Cashtown from Chambersburg, accompanied by Longstreet and I Corps. But before long they heard the rumble of artillery to the east; Lee grew anxious and rode ahead.

About three miles from Gettysburg, Lee passed through Pender's division of Hill's corps, deployed for battle. Farther on, at Herr Ridge, Lee found Heth still trying to re-form his shaken division after its earlier trial. To his front, the commanding general could see the brigades of Daniel and Ramseur fiercely engaged. General Heth, eager to redeem himself, asked permission to attack. "No," replied Lee, "I am not prepared to bring on a general engagement today — Longstreet is not up."

But Lee soon saw a cloud of dust beyond the right flank of the Federal XI Corps; Jubal Early and his division had arrived on the battlefield. Here was opportunity indeed. The long, thin, discontinuous Federal line was bent at a right angle, with XI Corps stretching from east to west and I Corps from north to south. Early was now assailing the Federal right, and Rodes was hammering at the vertex of the angle. If A. P. Hill could renew the assault against the Federal left, the

at the railroad cut in a lethal stalemate.

At the same time, Ramseur's brigade was having its own troubles against the stubborn troops of John Robinson's division. Robinson had sent a brigade under Brigadier General Gabriel René Paul to join Baxter's men near the Mummasburg road. Rodes, for his part, had neglected to alert Ramseur that Iverson had been ambushed there, and Ramseur's 1,027 men almost met the same fate. Warned at the last minute by two of Iverson's surviving officers, Ramseur adjusted his line of march to the east to strike the right flank of Paul's brigade. But nothing came easily to the Confederates on this afternoon — the Federals fought like furies.

In the struggle, General Paul suffered a head wound that left him blind and partly deaf. The officer who took over from him soon fell, and then others went down. Paul's brigade was led by five successive commanders. Baxter's brigade exhausted its ammunition and was forced to retire; when Paul's brigade ran low in turn, General Robinson went around scrounging cartridges from the dead and wounded. Finally, Paul's brigade

enemy would be caught as in the jaws of a nutcracker. Lee saw that it must be done. He ordered Heth, supported by Pender's division, to attack.

East of Oak Hill, General Doles had bided his time while Rodes fed the division's other brigades piecemeal into the battle. Expecting Early at any moment, Doles extended his line to meet him, sending skirmishers to seize a hillock near the County Alms House just to the west of the Heidlersburg road.

On the far right of the Federal XI Corps, Brigadier General Francis Barlow thought that same small prominence on the otherwise featureless plain looked like a good place to anchor his right flank. Quickly, Barlow's division of 2,459 men shouldered Doles's skirmishers off the hillock — which would thereafter be known as Barlow's Knoll.

In attacking, however, Barlow moved well ahead of the adjacent Federal division under Schimmelfennig. In order to correct the XI Corps alignment, General Schurz ordered Schimmelfennig forward. Inevitably, the movement triggered fighting, which swiftly grew in intensity.

Doles's single brigade of 1,323 men was soon engaged with two Federal divisions that totaled 5,530 troops, and his effort seemed doomed — until Early announced his arrival with a devastating explosion of cannon fire.

On Early's right, Brigadier General John B. Gordon's brigade struck Barlow's line from the front. The dashing Gordon led his men, waving his hat and standing in his stirrups on a coal-black stallion whose warlike appearance impressed a Confederate artillerist, even in the midst of chaos: "I never saw a horse's neck so arched, his eyes so fierce, his nostrils so dilated." Meanwhile, brigades

A lifelong friendship between Brigadier Generals Francis Barlow of the Union (*left*) and John Gordon of the Confederacy (*right*) began on the battlefield north of Gettysburg when Gordon came to the aid of the critically wounded Barlow. Both men survived the battle, but each thought the other had been killed at Gettysburg until they met by chance in Washington after the War. "Nothing short of resurrection from the dead could have amazed either of us more," wrote Gordon.

commanded by Brigadier General Harry T. Hays and Colonel Isaac E. Avery attacked down both sides of the Heidlersburg road, turning Barlow's right flank.

Barlow's position was utterly untenable. Moreover, his troops proved unreliable. "The enemy's skirmishers had hardly attacked us before my men began to run," Barlow later wrote. And back toward Gettysburg they went.

Riding after the retreating Federals, Gordon came upon an enemy officer lying dreadfully wounded with a Minié ball in his chest. Gordon dismounted, knelt to give him water and asked his name. "Francis C. Barlow," said the man, requesting that Gordon send word to Mrs. Barlow that her husband's dying thoughts had been of her. Gordon scribbled the note and sent it into Gettysburg under a white flag. Then, after having Barlow carried to the shade of a tree,

General Gordon went back to the fighting.

Barlow survived, but the collapse of his division sent shock waves along the entire Federal line; one by one the other units of XI Corps gave way to the Confederates and streamed toward Gettysburg. Watching, one of Early's officers sensed a triumph beyond reckoning: "It looked indeed as if the end of the war had come."

Yet over on the Federal left, against all hope or expectation, the men of Doubleday's I Corps still clung to McPherson's Ridge.

Moments after Lee granted permission for the attack, Heth's infantry had moved down the long incline of Herr Ridge toward Doubleday's lines. On the left, near the turnpike, was a Confederate brigade led by Colonel John M. Brockenbrough; in the center, facing the formidable task of clearing the Iron Brigade out of McPherson's Woods, were the men of James Pettigrew's brigade; on the right was Archer's bruised brigade, now commanded by Colonel Birkett D. Fry. The remnants of Davis' brigade, in no condition to fight, remained in the rear.

Although Heth was known for his bad luck, on this afternoon he was fortunate indeed. His clerk had adapted a civilian hat to Heth's use by rolling a dozen or so sheets of paper into the sweatband to achieve a proper fit. Just after crossing Willoughby Run, Heth was struck in the head by a Minié ball that fractured his skull and knocked him senseless; but for the rolled-paper padding, he might well have been killed.

With Pettigrew assuming command, the gray line pressed on toward McPherson's Ridge under heavy artillery and musket fire. From the woods, Colonel Henry A. Morrow of the Iron Brigade's 24th Michigan saw the men of the 26th North Carolina coming toward him, "yelling like demons."

"The fighting was terrible," reported Confederate Major J. T. Jones. "The two lines were pouring volleys into each other at a distance not greater than 20 paces." The North Carolina color-bearers were particularly hard hit. The brigade's assistant inspector general, Captain W. W. McCreery, seized the flag from a dying soldier and ran forward; he was shot through the heart and died instantly. Lieutenant George Wilcox of Company H picked up the bloody banner; he was killed seconds later.

Next, 21-year-old Henry King Burgwyn, the youngest colonel in the Confederate Army, raised the bullet-riddled flag. Knowing his commander risked certain death, Private Frank Honeycutt broke from the ranks and asked Burgwyn for the flag. At that moment both men went down, fatally wounded. Seeing them fall, the second-in-command of the 26th, Lieutenant Colonel John R. Lane, sprinted through the hail of fire and picked up the flag. When one of his lieutenants tried to stop him, Lane said grimly, "It is my time to take them now." Shouting, "Twenty-sixth, follow me!" he led the cheering Carolinians into the ranks of the Iron Brigade, which gave way before them. At the moment of victory, Lane too went down, severely wounded in the head. He was the 14th color-bearer in the regiment to fall that day.

Flanked on the left, the I Corps line fell back, fighting savagely before retiring to Seminary Ridge. Behind them in McPherson's Woods the bodies of men in blue and in gray lay intermingled.

The toll for both sides was staggering. During its day-long defense of McPherson's Ridge, the 1,829-man Iron Brigade had suffered 1,153 casualties; Heth's 7,500-man division had lost nearly 1,500. At the center of the caldron, Morrow's 24th Michigan had suffered 397 casualties, or just over 80 per cent of its 496 men. In the 26th North Carolina, only 212 of 800 men survived unwounded — a casualty rate of nearly 75 per cent —

and every one of the 90 officers and men of its Company F had fallen.

Riding into the woods after the Federal retreat, Pettigrew's assistant adjutant general, Captain Louis G. Young, heard the "dreadful — not moans but howls — of some of the wounded. It was so distressing that I approached several with the purpose of calming them if possible. I found them foaming at the mouth as if mad."

Back on Seminary Ridge, I Corps re-formed behind some crude breastworks that had been thrown up earlier. But before the exhausted men could catch their breath, William Dorsey Pender's division — a crack outfit led by one of the Confederacy's most promising young generals — was upon them.

Battery B of the 4th U.S. Artillery, commanded by Lieutenant James Stewart, managed to check the assault for a few minutes with double charges of canister. But then the Confederates came on again, charging over the bleeding bodies of their comrades. "Up and down the line," wrote one of Stewart's cannoneers with kaleidoscopic memory, "men reeling and falling; splinters flying from wheels and axles where bullets hit; in rear, horses tearing and plunging, mad with wounds or terror; drivers yelling, shells bursting, shot shrieking overhead, howling about our ears or throwing up great clouds of dust where they struck; the musketry crashing on three sides of us; bullets hissing, humming and whistling everywhere. Smoke, dust, splinters, blood, wreck and carnage indescribable."

In a trickle at first and then in a flood, I Corps broke again and fled from Seminary Ridge. Many of the soldiers mingled with the XI Corps throng in Gettysburg, others slanted to the southeast and the crest of Ceme-

At 3 p.m. on July 1, Lee's army began launching the heaviest assaults of the battle thus far. The divisions of Early and Rodes drove on Howard's XI Corps from the north while Pender and Heth were attacking Doubleday's I Corps from the west. Under pressure from the Confederates, XI and then I Corps gave way and withdrew through Gettysburg to positions on Cemetery Hill, Culp's Hill and Cemetery Ridge south of town.

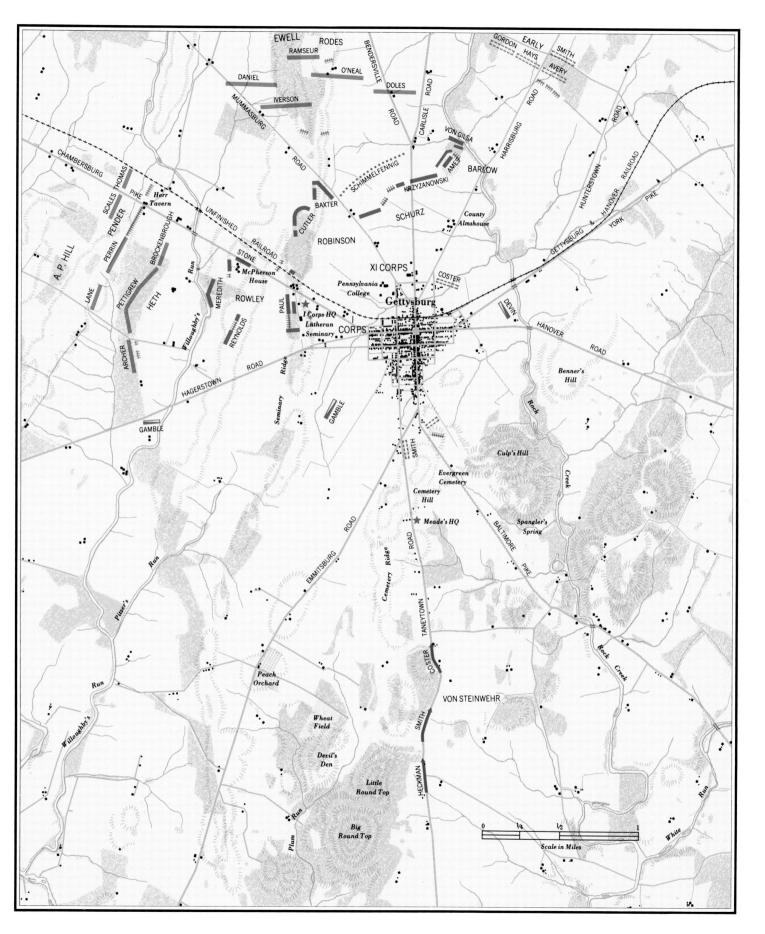

EWELL RODES

RAMSEUR

DANIEL O'NEAL

IVERSON DOLES

GORDON EARLY SMITH
HAYS
AVERY

BENDERSVILLE ROAD

CARLISLE ROAD

VON GILSA

CHAMBERSBURG PIKE

SCALES THOMAS

Herr Tavern

SCHIMMELFENNIG

AMES

BARLOW

HARRISBURG ROAD

HUNTERSTOWN ROAD

A. P. HILL

PENDER

PERRIN

BROCKENBROUGH

UNFINISHED

BAXTER

KRZYZANOWSKI

SCHURZ

County Almshouse

GETTYSBURG & HANOVER RAILROAD

YORK PIKE

LANE

PETTIGREW

HETH

Willoughby's Run

STONE

RAILROAD

CUTLER

ROBINSON

XI CORPS

COSTER

Pennsylvania College

McPherson House

ARCHER

MEREDITH

ROWLEY

PAUL

Gettysburg

DEVIN

REYNOLDS

I Corps HQ
Lutheran Seminary

CORPS

HANOVER ROAD

HAGERSTOWN ROAD

Seminary Ridge

GAMBLE

Benner's Hill

GAMBLE

SMITH

Culp's Hill

Rock Creek

Evergreen Cemetery

Cemetery Hill

Spangler's Spring

Meade's HQ

BALTIMORE PIKE

Pitzer's Run

EMMITSBURG ROAD

Cemetery Ridge

TANEYTOWN ROAD

Rock Creek

Willoughby's Run

Peach Orchard

COSTER

VON STEINWEHR

Wheat Field

SMITH

Devil's Den

Little Round Top

HECKMAN

Plum Run

Big Round Top

White Run

0   ¼   ½   1
Scale in Miles

The sole civilian known to have fought at Gettysburg was 72-year-old cobbler John Burns, who offered his services to the 150th Pennsylvania Volunteers. Wounded, he became a national hero, sought out by Lincoln and eulogized in verse by Bret Harte: "John Burns, a practical man / Shouldered his rifle, unbent his brows / And then went back to his bees and his cows."

The only recorded civilian fatality at Gettysburg was 20-year-old Jennie Wade, who was standing in her sister's kitchen kneading dough when a skirmisher's bullet pierced two wooden doors and killed her instantly. Her body was carried to the cellar by Federal soldiers; she was later buried in a coffin built by Confederate troops for one of their officers.

tery Hill, where Adolph von Steinwehr had been erecting defenses ever since his arrival.

There the Federals learned that yet another general had assumed command of the Gettysburg battlefield — and unlike Doubleday or Howard, this one was an inspiration to all the Federals. At 39, Winfield Scott Hancock was an officer of magnetic presence. "One felt safe when near him," a Federal officer recalled. Meade shared the high regard in which Hancock was held; on receiving the news of Reynolds' death, Meade had ordered Hancock to hurry north from Taneytown and take command of the field.

Arriving around 4:30 p.m., Hancock saw the Federal troops stampeding out of town and toward Cemetery Hill. "Wreck, disaster, disorder," one of his subordinates wrote later, "the panic that precedes disorganization, defeat and retreat were everywhere."

At the gate of the Evergreen Cemetery, Hancock met Howard, who was trying furiously to stop the rout. Howard was senior to Hancock, and their confrontation was awkward. Hancock explained that Meade had sent him to take charge, but Howard refused to yield. "You cannot give orders here," he said. "I am in command and I rank you."

Somehow, the two worked out a way of sharing command. Surveying the terrain, Hancock said carefully, "I think this is the strongest position by nature on which to fight a battle that I ever saw, and if it meets with your approbation I will select this as the battlefield." Howard agreed, and Hancock declared: "Very well, sir. I select this as the battlefield."

The field was in fact a topographic complex of which Cemetery Hill, rising about 80 feet above the town, was only a part. Just to the east stood Culp's Hill, about 100 feet higher, strewn with boulders and thick with woods. Stretching southward from Cemetery Hill for about two miles was the low Cemetery Ridge, dipping in places almost to ground level. At the southern end of Cemetery Ridge loomed two more hills — Little Round Top and, beyond it, Big Round Top.

Hancock was right: It was indeed a strong position. But it was also a long one, extending for nearly three miles; reinforcements would be needed to hold it. Major General Daniel E. Sickles' III Corps and Major General Henry W. Slocum's XII Corps were in fact on the way; whether they would arrive in time was another question.

Pending their arrival, Hancock set up a defensive line on Cemetery Hill facing to the north and west. Then he ordered Doubleday to send part of I Corps over to Culp's Hill. Doubleday protested that his men had been fighting all day and were completely done in. "Sir!" roared Hancock, rising in his stirrups, "I am in command on this field. Send every man you have!" Doubleday complied, with the battered Iron Brigade.

Having done all he could until reinforcements arrived, Hancock sat down on a stone fence and gazed through his field glasses at Seminary Ridge — where General Lee was beset by problems.

Following Pender's attacking division, Lee had stopped on Seminary Ridge to watch the Federal retreat to Cemetery Hill. Lee recognized immediately the value of possessing that high ground and urged A. P. Hill to renew his attack. For all his combativeness, Hill declined; his troops were bloodied, tired and almost out of ammunition.

That left the matter up to Ewell. Without taking time for written orders, Lee sent an

aide, Major Walter Taylor, to tell Ewell that, with the Federals in headlong flight, it "was only necessary to press those people in order to secure possession of the heights." It was the commanding general's wish that Ewell should do so "if practicable."

While Lee was waiting for his orders to bring results, James Longstreet arrived well in advance of his troops. Like Lee, he surveyed the scene — but he perceived a vastly different opportunity.

This was the perfect chance, Longstreet asserted, to initiate the sort of tactical defensive that he thought Lee had agreed upon. The army must swing around the Federal left, Longstreet said, interposing itself between the Army of the Potomac and Washington. The Confederates could then take up a strong defensive position and confidently await the attack that must surely result

from the threat posed to the Federal capital. "No," Lee said, gesturing toward Cemetery Hill, "the enemy is there, and I am going to attack him there."

Longstreet argued: "If he is there, it is because he is anxious that we should attack him — a good reason, in my judgment, for not doing so." But Lee replied, "I am going to whip them or they are going to whip me."

Discouraged but determined to push his plan, Longstreet rejoined his troops, leaving the commanding general anxiously awaiting Ewell's assault. It was about 5:30 p.m., and at least three hours of fighting time remained before darkness. A half hour passed, then another and yet another. At last, his patience gone, Lee rode off toward Ewell's headquarters on the Carlisle road north of Gettysburg.

Ewell had been gripped that day by a curious mental inertia. Arriving at the front

In the chaos on Cemetery Hill, an exploding shell sends artillery horses crashing to the ground or rearing in wild-eyed fright. The remnants of the shattered I and XI Corps were scattered over the hill; had the Confederates pressed their attack, the Federals might have met with disaster.

during Rodes's attack, he had been little more than a spectator. Then, as the Federals retreated, both Early and Gordon had urged him to push his corps past Gettysburg and onto the hills. Ewell declined, saying to Gordon: "General Lee told me to come to Gettysburg and gave me no orders to go farther."

A few moments later, Ewell was riding into Gettysburg with Gordon when there was an ominous thud, and Ewell reeled in his saddle. "Are you hurt, sir?" Gordon asked. "No, no," Ewell replied. "It don't hurt a bit to be shot in a wooden leg."

Later, fierce old Brigadier General Isaac Trimble, who was serving temporarily as an aide to Ewell, begged permission to lead a force against Culp's Hill. When Ewell brushed the suggestion aside, Trimble stomped away in a rage.

Late in the afternoon, Taylor arrived with Lee's oral order to seize the high ground south of Gettysburg "if practicable" — a discretionary phrase that only further puzzled Ewell. This was the first engagement in which Ewell had served directly under Lee; always before he had answered to Stonewall Jackson, whose orders left no leeway at all.

At any rate, Ewell failed to seize the advantage. And by the time Lee arrived at Ewell's headquarters, Federal reinforcements — the corps of Slocum and Sickles — were streaming onto Cemetery Ridge, and the opportunity had vanished.

The Federal commander was as worried as Lee. As the entanglement around Gettysburg worsened, General Meade thought about falling back to the defensive line his engineers had laid out along Pipe Creek. But

Hancock arrived at Meade's headquarters in Taneytown at about 9 p.m. and assured him that Gettysburg was the place to fight the next day's battle. Shortly after 10 p.m., the untried commander of the Army of the Potomac rode north, along roads congested by troops and wagons.

A few hours after midnight, he reached the little graveyard on Cemetery Hill and summoned ranking officers to the gatekeeper's living quarters. Turning to Howard, he asked: "Well, Howard, what do you think? Is this the place to fight the battle?" Replied Howard, "I am confident we can hold this position." The other officers agreed.

"I am glad to hear you say so, gentlemen," said Meade. "I have already ordered the other corps to concentrate here — and it is too late to change."

Through the Valley of Death

"My dead and wounded were nearly as great in number as those still on duty. They literally covered the ground. The blood stood in puddles in some places on the rocks; the ground was soaked with the blood of as brave men as ever fell on the red field of battle."

COLONEL WILLIAM C. OATES, 15TH ALABAMA, AT LITTLE ROUND TOP

"The roll was called in low tones. In the dim light of the daybreak we could see our infantry in front of us astir, and looking a little farther out into the gloom we could see the enemy's gray pickets. The stillness of everything was oppressive. We felt that a few flashes of musketry would be a relief.

"But the daylight came on, the sun rose and mounted up higher and higher, and yet the enemy, though in plain sight, gave no sign of hostility. Our men looked at each other and asked, 'What does it mean?' "

Thus wrote Augustus Buell, a teen-age cannoneer whose I Corps battery overlooked the Gettysburg plain from the frowning northern brow of Cemetery Hill. He and his comrades would find out soon enough what it meant. For on this sultry morning of July 2, volcanic forces were building toward a colossal eruption.

After only about three hours' sleep, Robert E. Lee arose at 3:30 a.m. and immediately dispatched two officers—Captain Samuel R. Johnston of his staff and Major J. J. Clarke of Longstreet's—to reconnoiter in the direction of the Round Tops. An hour and a half later, the commanding general was on Seminary Ridge, anxiously surveying the dispositions of the Federals concentrated on Cemetery Hill. Their line did not seem to Lee to extend very far south along Cemetery Ridge, the low spine connecting the hill with the Round Tops.

General Longstreet, whose corps was still arriving in the the vicinity of Herr Tavern on the Chambersburg Pike, joined Lee to press his arguments again in favor of a wide swing around the enemy's left. Although the precise details of the conversation were never disclosed, Lee must have pointed out that without Jeb Stuart's cavalry to scout the route, the army would have to grope its way through unfamiliar territory and would risk being entrapped by the Federals. At any event, Lee again courteously but firmly rejected Longstreet's proposal.

An ailing A. P. Hill, whose corps was still in place along Seminary Ridge, soon joined the conversation along with his division commander Henry Heth. As the generals sat on a log to make plans, a nearby British observer, Lieutenant Colonel Arthur Fremantle, noted with keen interest that Longstreet and Hill were indulging in the quaint American habit of whittling on sticks.

Major General John Bell Hood arrived to report that his division would reach the battlefield shortly—minus Brigadier General Evander Law's Alabama brigade, which was still a few hours away. Close behind Hood's force was Major General Lafayette McLaws' division. Its arrival would complete the concentration of Longstreet's corps, with one exception: Major General George E. Pickett's division, which had been left behind to guard the army's supply train at Chambersburg, would not reach Gettysburg until late afternoon.

After a while, Lee began pacing. "The

The Maltese-cross shape of this badge worn by Lieutenant William O. Colt signifies that his regiment, the 83rd Pennsylvania, belonged to General George Sykes's V Corps, which helped save the Federal left on the second day at Gettysburg. Colt's 295-man unit struggled to defend Little Round Top, suffering 55 casualties.

general is a little nervous this morning," Longstreet confided to Hood. "He wishes me to attack. I do not wish to do so without Pickett. I never like to go into battle with one boot off."

When McLaws arrived at about 9 a.m., he stepped unknowingly into a strained situation. "I wish you to place your division across this road," Lee said, pointing on a map to the Emmitsburg road, which ran southwestward from Cemetery Hill. "I wish you to get there if possible without being seen by the enemy. Can you do it?"

Plainly, until he had looked over the lay of the land, McLaws had no way of knowing whether he could do it. When he suggested that he reconnoiter, Longstreet, his corps commander, replied brusquely: "No, sir. I do not wish you to leave your division." Indicating a spot on the map, Longstreet told McLaws, "I wish your division placed so."

"No, General," said Lee, "I wish it placed just opposite." It was a tense and confusing little tiff that cast a long shadow over the day. Whether Longstreet was smarting because his flanking strategy had been overruled or was simply piqued because Lee had not observed the chain of command in issuing instructions directly to McLaws, the corps commander's mood remained black.

Captain Johnston returned from his scouting expedition to report that only Federal pickets occupied the southern portion of Cemetery Ridge and that the Round Tops were unoccupied. The news confirmed Lee's impression that the Federals were defending only the northernmost section of the ridge, and on that assumption he completed his plans for attack.

Longstreet would march to the south, then advance his two divisions along the Emmitsburg road to the northeast, toward Cemetery Ridge. After rolling up the Federal left, he would attack Cemetery Hill from the south, while A. P. Hill would assault Cemetery Hill from the west with the divisions of Major Generals Richard H. Anderson and William Dorsey Pender.

Lee ordered that the attack be made in echelon, starting on the right and moving toward the left, with one brigade after another striking the Federal line in a series of triphammer blows.

Ewell's corps, still in Gettysburg facing the Federal positions to the south, was to demonstrate in force at the first sound of Longstreet's guns. If the opportunity presented itself, he would make a full-scale assault on Cemetery Hill and Culp's Hill.

Lee's arrangements for these complicated operations were incredibly casual. He issued no written orders. At no time during the battle would he bring together his three corps commanders, upon whose understanding and cooperation the entire affair depended. And the commanding general would frequently act as his own courier, riding back and forth between Longstreet, Hill and Ewell at considerable cost of time.

In fact, Lee seemed out of sorts during the battle, and some thought him sick. One officer who reported to Lee's headquarters noted that the commanding general was walking as if "he was weak and in pain." The officer was later told that Lee was suffering from severe diarrhea. But it may have been more serious than that. Back in March, Lee had been laid low for two weeks by what he described as "a good deal of pain in my chest, back and arms. It came on in paroxysms and was quite sharp." Doubtless this was the heart disease that would one day kill Lee.

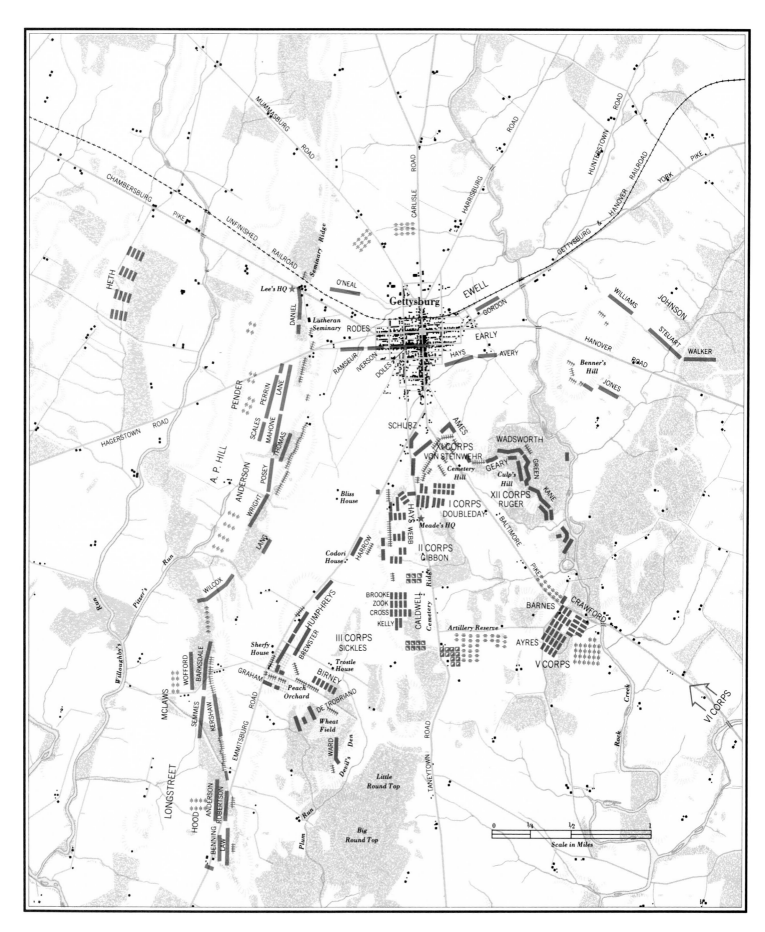

Shortly before 4 p.m. on July 2, John Bell Hood's division of Longstreet's corps launched the Confederate attack against the Federal left south of Gettysburg. About an hour later Lafayette McLaws' division joined in the attack, followed by Richard H. Anderson's division of A. P. Hill's corps. The Confederates captured the Devil's Den and smashed Sickles' III Corps in its exposed position in the Peach Orchard, but Federal reinforcements staved off a Confederate breakthrough.

General James Longstreet's disagreement with Robert E. Lee over tactics at Gettysburg did not affect their close friendship. "The relations existing between us were affectionate, confidential and even tender, from first to last," Longstreet later wrote. "There was never a harsh word between us."

And it is likely that he felt the pangs of the disease at Gettysburg, since only a few weeks after the battle he wrote to Jefferson Davis, "I have not yet recovered from the attack I experienced the past spring."

When Lee completed his plans on the morning of July 2, he turned to Longstreet and said, "I think you had better move on." It was about 10 a.m. Lee rode off to see Ewell, expecting Longstreet's assault to be under way by the time he returned. But after he found Ewell, talked with him briefly and started back toward his own headquarters, Lee still heard no gunfire and showed his exasperation. "What can detain Longstreet?" Lee exclaimed. "He ought to be in position now." Passing by Hill's front on Seminary Hill, Lee was joined by that general's artillery commander, Colonel R. Lindsay Walker. "As we rode together," Walker later recalled, "General Lee manifested more impatience than I ever saw him exhibit on any other occasion; he seemed very much disappointed and worried that the attack had not opened earlier."

To his dismay, Lee found that Longstreet had not even begun the march toward his attack position. Longstreet said he was waiting for Law's brigade; it did not arrive for another hour, and not until noon did the corps finally get under way.

Shortly after Longstreet began moving his men into position, the long-lost Jeb Stuart arrived at Gettysburg. He was riding far ahead of his men, who were returning from their wild and pointless foray (pages 72-73).

According to Stuart's adjutant, Major Henry McClellan, the meeting between Lee and Stuart that afternoon was "painful beyond description." At the sight of Stuart, Lee reddened, raised his hand as if to strike and demanded to know where Stuart had been. "I have not heard a word from you for days, and you the eyes and ears of my army."

"I have brought you 125 wagons and their teams, General," replied Stuart.

"Yes," said Lee, "and they are an impediment to me now."

Then the commanding general's manner turned from anger to "great tenderness," according to McClellan. "Let me ask your help now," Lee said, "We will not discuss this matter further. Help me fight these people." But it was already too late for Stuart's strung-out forces to join the assault that day.

Longstreet, meanwhile, had encountered nothing but frustration in trying to move his two divisions to the point of attack.

To avoid detection, he had first marched the men west on the Chambersburg Pike to the hamlet of Seven Stars. There they turned off on a narrow, winding country road that led south along Marsh Creek toward Black Horse Tavern on the Hagerstown road. At that point, McLaws' leading brigade, commanded by Brigadier General Joseph B. Kershaw, struck east toward the Emmits-burg road. Kershaw had gone only a few hundred yards, however, when he came to Herr Ridge and realized that his brigade would be seen by the enemy if it passed over the rise. He ordered a halt.

Longstreet came up, took a look from the crest and returned, as Kershaw recalled, "manifesting considerable irritation." Longstreet ordered his entire force to march

Jeb Stuart's Untimely Ride

Confederates pursue a fleeing wagon while their comrades halt others in the background.

On the morning of June 25, Confederate cavalry leader Jeb Stuart set out from Salem, Virginia, with three brigades of horsemen and rode eastward on a mission to scout and harass the Army of the Potomac. That evening, the troopers discovered to their surprise that a large segment of that army — General Winfield Scott Hancock's entire II Corps — was encamped directly astride Stuart's planned route.

Stuart's 4,800 men could not shoot their way through Hancock's large force. So Stuart faced two options: He could prudently ride back westward and maintain contact with Robert E. Lee's northbound army, or he could ride around Hancock. Characteristically, Stuart decided to follow the more daring course, taking his three brigades on a detour south and east before turning north. In doing so, he put two mountain ranges and the entire Federal army between himself and Lee's right flank.

Committed to his venture, Stuart rushed his troopers past Fairfax Court House and across the Potomac at Rowser's Ford, only a dozen miles from Washington, and then on to Rockville, Maryland.

There, the already weary troopers saw an invigorating sight — a huge Federal wagon train packed with supplies. "The wagons were brand new, the mules fat and sleek and the harness in use for the first time," a Confederate officer later wrote, still relishing the memory. "Such a train we had never seen before and did not see again."

The chase was on. Teamsters desperately turned their wagons and fled pell-mell back toward Washington. Stuart's men, howling in delight, rode them down (left). The take was bountiful: 900 mules, 400 prisoners of war, and 125 wagons full of food for the hungry troopers and fodder for their horses.

Ultimately, however, the captured supply train proved more of an encumbrance than a boon to Stuart. The mule-drawn wagons slowed the cavalry's daily pace from 40 to 25 miles — adding, as it turned out, two crucial days to an expedition that had already deprived General Lee of his best mounted scouts for a dangerously long time.

Leaving Rockville on June 28, the Confederate horsemen continued northward into Pennsylvania, cutting telegraph lines, tearing up railroad tracks — and fighting several fierce little battles with bands of Federal cavalry. In one skirmish, near Hanover, Stuart would have been captured or killed by Federal troopers had not he and his big mare, Virginia, escaped by leaping a deep, 15-foot-wide ditch; the two sailed over the ravine, a fellow officer recalled, with "Stuart's fine fig-

back toward the Chambersburg Pike; he then sent them down another route along Willoughby Run. Thus delayed by nearly two hours, his corps finally began filing into place west of the Emmitsburg road at about 3:30 p.m., with Hood's division on the right facing the Round Tops and McLaws' on the left opposite Cemetery Ridge.

McLaws had been told to expect little or no opposition on his immediate front. But just to make sure, he rode forward, dismounted and walked to the edge of the woods in which his division was concealed. "The view presented astonished me," he wrote later, "as the enemy was massed in my front, and extended to my right and left as far as I could see."

The large Federal force deployed along

---

ure sitting erect and firm in the saddle."

Still, there seemed no way to turn westward without encountering large units of the Federal army. Stuart's only chance was to press on to York or even distant Carlisle, hoping to link up with Lee's advance corps under Richard Ewell. The troopers slept in their saddles, many falling off and thudding onto the dusty road. Nearing York on June 30, Stuart found that Jubal Early's division of Ewell's corps had been there but had left hurriedly. Stuart pushed his men mercilessly onward in pursuit.

Arriving near Carlisle at last on July 1, Stuart's advance guard discovered that the town was not in Confederate hands but was held by Federal militia under General William F. Smith. The crusty Smith refused, in salty language, to surrender, so Stuart shelled the town (below) and set fire to Carlisle's cavalry barracks. Late that night a courier — one of eight sent out by Lee to scour the Pennsylvania countryside for Stuart — rode up with news of fierce fighting at Gettysburg. At 1 a.m. on July 2, Jeb Stuart began another night ride, galloping south to report to his anxious chief.

A Federal officer rides through Carlisle (center) as shells explode, wounding several New York and Philadelphia militiamen.

the Emmitsburg road only 600 yards away was General Daniel Sickles' III Corps — and its presence there was almost as unpleasant a surprise to the commander of the Army of the Potomac as it was to General McLaws.

General Meade had been up all night, inspecting and arranging his lines. At 8 a.m., General Carl Schurz of XI Corps encountered him on Cemetery Hill; to Schurz, Meade was looking "careworn and tired." Schurz asked how many men Meade had at his disposal. "In the course of the day," Meade replied, "I expect to have about 95,000 — enough, I expect, for this business." Then, with an air of resignation, he added: "Well, we may as well fight it out here as anywhere else."

During the night and early morning, the roads from the south had been thronged by hard-marching Federal troops, many of whom had not slept for two days. By 9 a.m., most of the Army of the Potomac was present, deployed in the shape of a rough horseshoe pointing toward Gettysburg and open to the south. On the Federal right, Slocum's XII Corps held a line along the rocky slope extending southeast from Culp's Hill along Rock Creek. The arc of the horseshoe was manned by Wadsworth's battered I Corps division on Culp's Hill and Howard's shaky XI Corps on Cemetery Hill.

Behind XI Corps on Cemetery Hill were the other two I Corps divisions — feeling somewhat disgruntled. The day before, upon receiving Howard's misleading report that I Corps had ignominiously fled from the field, Meade had relieved Doubleday. Major General John Newton of VI Corps took over I Corps, and some of the soldiers were complaining. One of them later wrote that Dou-

Brigadier General Evander M. Law, seated at center with his staff, lodged a formal protest against the Confederate plan of attack before leading his Alabama brigade in the assault on Little Round Top. The Federal position, he later wrote, "was practically impregnable to attack."

bleday, during his brief try at corps command, had "displayed skill and courage which the dullest private could not help commending. The men considered Doubleday entitled to command of the corps, and they were disgusted when they learned that a stranger had been put over them."

At Cemetery Hill, Meade's line bent sharply southward, with Hancock's II Corps extending down Cemetery Ridge. Sickles was ordered to position III Corps beyond Hancock on the extreme Federal left.

Meade's old V Corps, now under Major General George Sykes, was posted in reserve on the Baltimore Pike behind Cemetery Hill, a location that gave easy access to all parts of the battlefield.

Major General John Sedgwick's VI Corps — at nearly 14,000 men the army's largest — had yet to arrive. On the evening of July 1, Sedgwick had been at Manchester, 30 miles southeast of Gettysburg, worried mostly about keeping his men away from the ample supplies of local whiskey. Just before sunset, a courier galloped up to Sedgwick's headquarters with dispatches from Meade describing the day's events and urging haste in bringing VI Corps up. Sedgwick looked at his watch. "Tell General Meade," he said, "that my corps will be at Gettysburg at 4 o'clock tomorrow." It would mean marching all night and most of the next day, but John Sedgwick would keep his appointment.

Meade's dispositions at Gettysburg reflected his deep concern about the large numbers of enemy troops visible to the north and northeast; to meet that threat, he had stationed the better part of three corps on or near Cemetery and Culp's Hills, with still another corps in reserve. His view of the Confederates and their movements to the west, on the other hand, was obscured by ridges and woods. Meade discounted the possibility of an attack from that direction and stretched his II and III Corps thin along the low spine of Cemetery Ridge.

This was, of course, a calculated risk. In fact, his left wing was even weaker than Meade realized. The previous evening Brigadier General John W. Geary's division of XII Corps had been sent south on Cemetery Ridge, and two of Geary's regiments had spent the night on Little Round Top.

At 5 a.m. on July 2, Geary was ordered to join the rest of the corps at Culp's Hill; he was to be relieved on Cemetery Ridge by Sickles' III Corps.

Geary, a Mexican War veteran, recognized that if the Confederates possessed Little Round Top they would have, in his words, "an opportunity of enfilading our entire left wing and center with a fire which could not fail to dislodge us." Before departing, then, Geary sent an aide to Sickles with a note explaining the critical importance of the position. Sickles shrugged it off, saying only that he would "attend to it in due time." Geary waited a while, then sent another message; Sickles ignored it. Geary could delay no longer, and he left Little Round Top undefended — a fact that Captain Johnston would soon report to General Lee.

At 6 a.m., General Meade sent an aide — his son and namesake George — to see if III Corps was properly placed. Captain Meade returned to report that Sickles was not certain where his troops were supposed to be posted. Dispatched again to tell Sickles to hold the line recently vacated by Geary, Captain Meade found Sickles inspecting the terrain with displeasure. Yet it was not Little Round Top that concerned him.

A half mile north of the Round Tops, Cemetery Ridge diminished in height until it was a barely perceptible swell in the countryside. Sickles thought this low place a feeble position, rendered even more vulnerable by the fact that it was commanded by higher ground — upon which a peach orchard was situated — about half a mile to the west. Enemy guns on that elevation would imperil the III Corps line, Sickles said, and he requested that General Meade come to look over his situation. When midmorning passed with no word, Sickles rode over to see the army commander.

Meade had little respect for Sickles, and his response had a cutting edge. "Oh," he scoffed, "generals are apt to look for the attack to be made where they are." Undaunted, Sickles asked if he was authorized to use his own judgment in placing his men. Replied Meade: "Certainly, within the limits of the general instructions I have given you; any ground within those limits you choose to occupy I leave to you."

Meade sent the army's artillery chief, Brigadier General Henry J. Hunt, back with Sickles to survey the situation. To the gunner's keen eye, the elevation out in front of the Federal left—the Peach Orchard, as it would henceforth be known—was attractive. It was a short, flat-topped ridge, midway between Cemetery and Seminary Ridges and traversed diagonally by the Emmitsburg road. From the orchard, another ridge ran off to the southeast, terminating after about 1,100 yards in a fantastic jumble of huge granite boulders called the Devil's Den. Between the Devil's Den and Little Round Top, 500 yards to the east, was a marshy, rock-strewn swale that would soon be known as the Valley of Death; through it flowed a little stream named Plum Run.

General Hunt agreed that the Peach Orchard ridge and the one leading to the Devil's Den "constituted a favorable position for the enemy to hold." He added: "This was one good reason for our taking possession of it." But when Sickles asked if he should advance his corps, Hunt temporized. "Not on my authority," he said. "I will report to General Meade for his instructions." Then Hunt suggested that Sickles send out skirmishers to find out if there actually were Confederate

The courageous and skillful commanding officer of the 20th Maine, Joshua Chamberlain, was a professor of rhetoric, oratory and modern languages at Bowdoin College when he volunteered for service at the age of 33 in 1862. After the War, Chamberlain was elected governor of Maine and later became Bowdoin's president.

troops in the thickets, called Pitzer's Woods, beyond the Emmitsburg road to his front.

Sickles quickly sent out four companies of the 1st U.S. Sharpshooters, supported by the 3rd Maine Regiment. The sharpshooters—handsomely clad in dark green uniforms and leather leggings—were part of an elite outfit led by Colonel Hiram Berdan.

Across the Emmitsburg road, Berdan's men ran into Confederate skirmishers, drove them back and then came up against stiff resistance. After a brisk fire fight, Berdan pulled out and reported to Sickles: Pitzer's Woods were indeed full of Confederates. In fact, the Confederates were only three regiments of General Cadmus Wilcox's Alabama brigade—the far right of Hill's corps. Longstreet's corps was still miles away. But Sick-

William C. Oates, commander of the 15th Alabama, described himself as having been "born in poverty" and "reared in adversity." Forced to leave his home at the age of 16 because of a scrape with the law, Oates labored as an itinerant house painter; he nevertheless managed to gain an education and became an attorney before volunteering in 1861. He later served in the Alabama legislature, in the U.S. House of Representatives and as Alabama's governor.

les did not know this, and he determined to advance en masse to the Emmitsburg road. At 3 p.m., the 10,000 battle-tested veterans of III Corps pushed forward, skirmishers in front, artillery to the rear, colors flapping, swords and bayonets gleaming, drums beating a steady tattoo.

"How splendidly they march!" exclaimed an admiring II Corps soldier, watching from farther north on Cemetery Ridge. Said another: "It looks like a dress parade, a review." But the II Corps commander, General Winfield Scott Hancock, was less admiring; he realized that Sickles was not only isolating his corps a half mile in front of the rest of the army but had exposed the left flank of II Corps. "Wait a moment," Hancock said to the officers gathered around

him. "You will see them tumbling back."

General Meade, unaware of Sickles' redeployment, summoned his corps commanders to a council of war. Sickles sent word that he was too busy to attend. Meade sent a peremptory order summoning Sickles, and after a while he rode up, just as the booming of guns was heard to the south. "General, I will not ask you to dismount," said Meade. "The enemy is engaging your front. The council is over." Sickles hastily left.

Having neglected his left wing all day, Meade reacted quickly to the sound of battle there. He instructed Sykes to hurry V Corps up from the Baltimore Pike in support of Sickles; VI Corps would take the place of Sykes's corps in reserve. Then Meade rode out to make a personal reconnaissance of the endangered left.

With him went the army's chief topographical engineer, Brigadier General Gouverneur Kemble Warren. Warren was an emotional man, with the soulful eyes of a poet; he was also endowed with an excellent feel for ground and an abundance of good sense. Meade trusted him completely and sent him off to make sure that troops had been posted on the hills at the southern end of Cemetery Ridge.

When Meade arrived under heavy artillery fire at Sickles' III Corps line, he must have shuddered at what he saw. There, far out in front and aligned along the Emmitsburg road with its right flank completely exposed, was the division of Brigadier General Andrew A. Humphreys. On Humphreys' left, Brigadier General David B. Birney's division occupied the Peach Orchard, then angled off on a line to the southeast, stretching past a wheat field to the Devil's Den and the Plum Run Valley beyond. Thus, the two divisions formed a salient that could be vulnerable to fire from two sides.

When Meade found Sickles in the Peach Orchard, the army commander could barely restrain his temper. "General," said Meade, "I am afraid you are too far out." When Sickles tried to explain that he had gained the advantage of higher ground, Meade sarcastically interrupted: "General Sickles, this is in some respects higher ground than that to the rear, but there is still higher in front of you, and if you keep on advancing you will find constantly higher ground all the way to the mountains."

By then, Sickles himself was having some second thoughts. But just as he offered to withdraw his corps to its original position, a shell burst nearby. "I wish to God you could," Meade shouted, "but those people will not permit it." The words were hardly out of Meade's mouth when his horse Baldy, maddened by the shellfire, bolted and galloped off, carrying Meade some distance to the rear before the general could bring his mount under control.

The Confederate commanders had been having their own disagreements. Confronted by Sickles' newly arrived troops, General McLaws immediately realized that Lee's plan by chance had been knocked askew. Instead of thrusting along an undefended Emmitsburg road toward a weak Federal flank on Cemetery Ridge, as Lee had envisioned, McLaws would have to fight every inch of the way. But when McLaws sent word to Longstreet of the changed situation, he received a disdainful reply: "There is no one in your front but a regiment of infantry and a battery of artillery." Twice more McLaws protested — and twice more he was told that

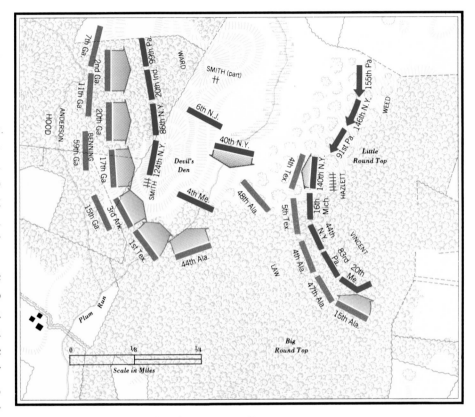

he must attack when the time came. Days later, still resentful, McLaws wrote to his wife that Longstreet had been "exceedingly overbearing."

General John Bell Hood was enduring similar frustrations on the Confederate far right. From his attack position in the woods, Hood could see Birney's Federals in the Peach Orchard salient to the northeast. And Hood's scouts reported that although the Round Tops were unoccupied, the enemy's line extended all the way to the Devil's Den.

Thus, if Hood followed Lee's orders to make an assault to the north, his troops would take devastating fire from the right. Hood was brave to the point of recklessness, but he knew, as he wrote later, that even if this "feat was accomplished, it must be at a most fearful sacrifice." It would be far bet-

On the south flank at Gettysburg, Evander Law's Alabamians attacked Strong Vincent's brigade on Little Round Top while Henry Benning's Georgians and Jerome Robertson's Texas brigade hammered their way through the Devil's Den and past Plum Run, beating back Hobart Ward's Federal brigade of III Corps. Two regiments of Robertson's Texans then attacked Stephen Weed's brigade on Little Round Top.

ter, Hood reasoned, to take his division around the southern edge of Round Top and strike the enemy's line on Cemetery Ridge from the flank and rear. Hood sent a messenger to urge this course of action on his corps commander.

Longstreet's answer was brief and unequivocal: "General Lee's orders are to attack up the Emmitsburg road." The more Hood looked up that road, the less he liked it. Again, he asked Longstreet to allow him to swing around the Round Tops. Again, Longstreet replied: "General Lee's orders are to attack up the Emmitsburg road."

Never before in his military career had Hood protested the orders of a superior of-

ficer. Now he did, advancing his plan for a third time. Longstreet's answer was the same. This time, however, Longstreet rode over to Hood's position to say, "We must obey the orders of General Lee."

In the end, Hood simply ignored Longstreet. In clear disregard of his orders, he faced his division eastward and launched an attack in the direction of the Devil's Den and the Round Tops, hoping to outflank the Federal left.

Hood's division advanced in two lines. On the right front was Evander Law's Alabama brigade, supported about 200 yards behind by the Georgia brigade of Brigadier General Henry L. Benning. To the left was Hood's

Confederate dead lie among the boulders and shell-scarred trees in the Plum Run area, later called the Valley of Death. A soldier in the 5th Texas recalled being in the midst of the fighting: "The balls are whizzing so thick that it looks like a man could hold out a hat and catch it full."

old Texas brigade, now commanded by Brigadier General Jerome B. Robertson; it was backed by another Georgia brigade under Brigadier General George T. Anderson.

As the troops advanced, the 15th Alabama, on the far right of Law's line, came under heavy fire from the 2nd U.S. Sharpshooters on the heavily wooded lower slope of Big Round Top. To clear them out, the 15th Alabama and most of the 47th Alabama charged up the hill.

It was a cruel climb, recalled Colonel William C. Oates, commander of the 15th. His men were "catching to the rocks and bushes and crawling over the boulders in the face of the fire of the enemy, who kept retreating, taking shelter and firing down on us from behind the rocks and crags which covered the side of the mountain thicker than gravestones in a city cemetery." About halfway up, the enemy resistance faded away. At length Oates's men arrived, sobbing for breath, on the summit of Big Round Top, 305 feet above the plain, the highest place for miles around.

Oates let his men rest for a few minutes while he surveyed the scene to the north. Through the foliage, he could see all the way to Cemetery and Culp's Hills. There, and down the crest of Cemetery Ridge, Federal troops were digging in; to his immediate front, on Little Round Top more than 100 feet below him, a few Federal signalmen were wigwagging their semaphore flags.

Then and for the rest of his life, William Oates was convinced that at that moment he held the key to Gettysburg. If a few artillery pieces could somehow be manhandled up Big Round Top and a field of fire cleared by axmen, the Confederates would possess what Oates called "a Gibraltar that I

could hold against ten times the number of men that I had." And from that height, the guns could blast the enemy line from one end to the other.

As Oates contemplated this exhilarating prospect, Captain L. R. Terrell of Evander Law's staff arrived, having somehow ridden up the hill on horseback. Terrell reported that General Hood had been wounded — his arm shattered from biceps to wrist by a bursting shell — and Law was now in command of the division. Law's orders were for Oates to abandon his hard-won perch on Big Round Top and seize Little Round Top.

Oates descended the 500-yard-long saddle between the two hills. On the way, he and his men were joined on their left by Law's 4th Alabama and by the 4th and 5th Texas of Robertson's brigade; these units had worked around Devil's Den and the western base of Big Round Top. As Oates made his way across the saddle, not a single enemy soldier was in sight. But as the troops began to ascend the rugged southeastern slope of Little

General Gouverneur Warren, peering through field glasses from the crest of Little Round Top, sights the attacking Confederates. "The discovery," Warren later wrote, "was intensely thrilling to my feelings, and almost appalling."

Dashing down the southern slope of Little Round Top, the 20th Maine, led by Colonel Joshua Chamberlain (*sword raised, right of center*), counterattacks the 15th Alabama, under Colonel William C. Oates (*right foreground*). "Chamberlain's voice thrilled along the line," recalled a Maine man, "and the whole regiment swept forward with irresistible force."

Round Top, suddenly, without the slightest warning, from behind a natural barricade of rocks less than 50 steps to their front, poured what Oates would always remember as "the most destructive fire I ever saw."

The Federals behind the rocks had been there for only 10 minutes — about the same length of time that Oates had rested his men on Big Round Top. Their presence was attributable to the good judgment of chief engineer Gouverneur Warren, who had been sent by Meade to the Round Tops. Arriving just before the Confederate advance, Warren had found Little Round Top occupied only by those few signalmen, who nervously reported seeing movement in the woods near the Emmitsburg road. Warren had ordered Captain James Smith's 4th New York Battery above the Devil's Den to fire a shell into the area. The burst caused an instant stir in the timber. "The motion," Warren wrote later, "revealed to me the glistening of gun barrels and bayonets of the enemy's line of battle, already formed and far outflanking the position of any of our troops."

Now, suddenly, every minute was pre-cious. Warren sent an aide to Meade, requesting that at least one division be rushed to Little Round Top. Another staff officer, Lieutenant Ranald S. Mackenzie, galloped off to seek help from General Sickles. But Sickles replied that he needed every one of his men — which was certainly the truth, for a few minutes earlier, the reluctant McLaws had launched his attack.

In desperation, Mackenzie went to General Sykes, whose V Corps was moving forward to support Sickles. Sykes had a reputation for slowness that had earned him the nickname "Tardy George," but there was nothing slow about him on this day: He immediately sent one of his aides to find Brigadier General James Barnes, at 62 the army's oldest division commander, with orders to rush a brigade to the threatened hill.

Barnes was not with his division, and nobody seemed to know where he was. But Colonel Strong Vincent, commanding the brigade at the head of Barnes's column, called to the staff officer, "Captain, what are your orders?" Pointing to Little Round Top, the captain said: "General Sykes told me to direct General Barnes to send one

Riflemen of General Stephen Weed's brigade defend the western slope of Little Round Top against the last Confederate assault on the hill, delivered by two Texas regiments. "The air was saturated with the sulphurous fumes of battle and was ringing with the shouts and groans of the combatants," remembered an officer of the 140th New York.

of his brigades to occupy that hill yonder."

Colonel Vincent, a 26-year-old Harvard graduate and lawyer, was a stern disciplinarian who had gotten off to a bad start with his troops. One of his men had written: "I thought him a dude and an upstart." But in time the colonel had earned the respect and then the affection of his men, and now they would follow him anywhere—as they were about to demonstrate. "I will take the responsibility of taking my men there," Vincent told the captain. Then he led his brigade up the slope of Little Round Top and deployed his men among the rocks.

The last of Vincent's four regiments to gain the heights was the 20th Maine, a regiment of fishermen and lumberjacks who had learned how to fight and fight well. As they took their position, Vincent told their commander, Colonel Joshua Lawrence Chamberlain: "This is the left of the Union line." By that he meant the left of the entire Army of the Potomac. "You understand. You are to hold this ground at all costs."

Colonel Chamberlain understood perfectly—and for his work during the next hour and a half the 34-year-old former seminarian and professor of rhetoric at Bowdoin College would be awarded the Medal of Honor. No sooner had Chamberlain's men put their backs to the side of the hill than Oates and his Confederates appeared. From behind their protective rocks, the men of the 20th Maine rose, fired and sent the enemy line staggering back. The Confederates reformed and rushed again, against a hail of bullets so destructive that, in Oates's words, "my line wavered like a man trying to walk against a strong wind."

When the Alabamians began to lap around his left flank, Chamberlain ordered the left wing to drop back, so that the 20th Maine's formation took the shape of a V. The fighting, wrote Private Theodore Gerrish of the 20th Maine, became "a terrible medley of cries, shouts, cheers, groans, prayers, curses, bursting shells, whizzing rifle bullets and clanging steel. The air seemed to be alive with lead. The lines at times were so near each other that the hostile gun barrels almost touched." Colonel Oates's younger brother, Lieutenant John A. Oates, was hit and fell dying. The colonel cried: "Forward, my men, to the ledge!" And firing his revolver, he led a surge toward the Federal line 30 yards away.

"Again and again," wrote Captain Howard L. Prince of the 20th Maine, "this mad rush repeated, each time to be beaten off by the ever-thinning line that desperately clung to its ledge of rock." Chamberlain recalled that "the edge of the conflict swayed to and fro, with wild whirlpools and eddies. At times I saw around me more of the enemy than of my own men; gaps opening, swallowing, closing again with sharp convulsive energy. All around, a strange, mingled roar."

Now Chamberlain's dead lay sprawled grotesquely around him, his soldiers were down to their last cartridges and the Confederates were rallying for another charge. Chamberlain decided to fix bayonets and charge first. But his shouted orders could not be heard above the din, and the men stayed where they were. Then Lieutenant Holman S. Melcher of Company F jumped out in front of the line, yelled "Come on! Come on, boys!" and charged—alone. Moments passed, then a few men followed, then more, and then, with an animal roar, the entire 20th Maine, led by Chamberlain with drawn sword.

The shocked Confederates stopped, stumbled back and braced themselves. But suddenly they were hit from behind. The sharpshooters who had earlier opposed Oates's passage to the Round Tops were now firing on his rear; other Federals were on his flanks. "While one man was shot in the face," Oates wrote, "his right-hand or left-hand comrade was shot in the side or back. Some were struck simultaneously with two or three balls from different directions."

Two of Oates's junior officers urged withdrawal. Oates refused. "Return to your companies," he said. "We will sell out as dearly as possible." Then he changed his mind and passed the word for every man to get out as best he could. "When the signal was given," he said, "we ran like a herd of wild cattle."

The 20th Maine, at a cost of 130 of its 386 men, had won its lonely fight. But farther around the hill, on the west slope, the Federal troops were in desperate straits. There, on the far right of Vincent's brigade, the 16th Michigan was beginning to crumble under savage attack from Robertson's 4th and 5th Texas. As Colonel Vincent tried to rally the Michiganders, he went down mortally wounded, murmuring, "Don't give an inch." But just as all seemed lost for the Michigan men, reinforcements arrived, thanks again to General Warren.

Warren had continued his mission to get men and artillery onto Little Round Top. As the fighting there broke out, he helped Lieutenant Charles E. Hazlett and his gunners manhandle the guns of Battery D, 5th U.S. Artillery, to the crown of the hill. Then Warren descended from Little Round Top in quest of reinforcements.

The first outfit he came to was the 140th New York, the rearmost regiment of Briga-

dier General Stephen H. Weed's V Corps brigade, which was on its way to support Sickles. The New Yorkers were led by Colonel Patrick H. O'Rorke, a brilliant 27-year-old who had graduated first in the West Point class of June 1861.

Warren shouted that O'Rorke's men were badly needed on Little Round Top. O'Rorke, although always ready for a fight, explained that he was under orders to follow the rest of Weed's brigade. "Never mind that, Paddy," said Warren. "Bring them up on the double-quick and don't stop for aligning. I'll take the responsibility." That was sufficient. O'Rorke's men rushed to the crest

The Parrott guns of Lieutenant Charles Hazlett's Battery D, 5th U.S. Artillery, fire from the summit of Little Round Top. The guns were hauled up the steep hill "at a trot, with spurs and whips vigorously applied," recalled Lieutenant Benjamin Rittenhouse, who commanded the battery after Hazlett was killed. "The country on the left and front was full of rebels," Rittenhouse continued, "and coming so rapidly that it seemed almost impossible to stop them."

the artilleryman instructions for the payment of a few small debts he owed to fellow officers. Then, as if to whisper in Hazlett's ear, he drew his friend closer — and Hazlett was killed instantly by a bullet in his brain.

Weed was visited in a field hospital that night by an aide who tried to cheer him up. "General," he said, "I hope you're not so badly hurt." Replied Weed: "I'm as dead a man as Julius Caesar." A little later, he was.

The men on the summit of Little Round Top could see to the immediate west a savage battle for the Devil's Den and the Plum Run Valley. It was, wrote one of O'Rorke's officers, a vista "full of smoke and fire, and literally swarming with riderless horses and fighting, fleeing and pursuing men. The wild cries of charging lines, the rattle of musketry, the booming of artillery and the shrieks of the wounded were the orchestral accompaniments of a scene like very hell itself."

The Devil's Den — a wilderness of huge boulders piled without pattern, a labyrinth of crevices, caves and dank, dark, rock-walled passages — formed the base of the ridge that rose up toward the Peach Orchard. Near the crest of that ridge were positioned six guns of the 4th New York Battery under Captain James E. Smith, supported by Brigadier General Hobart Ward's brigade.

The Federals were New York, Pennsylvania, Maine and Indiana men. One of the regiments, the 124th New York, was made up of men from Orange County who wore orange ribbons on their coats and called themselves the "Orange Blossoms." Their commander was a hard-bitten 37-year-old colonel named Augustus Van Horne Ellis. He was described by one of his officers, Captain

of Little Round Top and plunged without pausing down its western face, smashing into Robertson's Texans and driving them back down the slope. Paddy O'Rorke was killed while leading the charge.

On learning of O'Rorke's departure, Weed had turned his three remaining regiments around and headed for Little Round Top. By the time he got there, the battle was almost over. Confederate snipers were still active, however; and one of their Minié balls passed through Weed from shoulder to shoulder, severing his spine. "I am cut in two," he groaned. "I want to see Hazlett." When his old friend came over, Weed gave

Charles Weygant, as "a rather cold, harsh, ambitious man who sometimes chilled us with his terrible bursts of profanity." But, as Weygant was quick to add: "In that indescribable soldierly quality which — for want of a better term — we shall call dash, he was unsurpassed by any officer in our Corps."

Before the Confederate attack, Smith's guns had engaged in a thunderous duel with enemy batteries — it was a shell from one of Smith's cannon that had wounded General Hood in the arm. And then, from the Federal ranks, a cry had arisen: "Here they come! Here they come!"

Jerome Robertson's Texas and Arkansas regiments, followed by Benning's Georgians, descended on the Federal positions. In the wild fight that followed, some of the Confederates assailed the Devil's Den, while others flooded into the Valley of

Death, where they were hit by the fire of Federal troops on Little Round Top. A private of the 4th Texas, Joe Smith, dipped a handkerchief in the murky water of Plum Run and wrapped it around his head to cool himself. The handkerchief was an inviting target — and Smith fell with a bullet through his skull.

Leading the 5th Texas across Plum Run and wresting a foothold on the slope of Little Round Top, Major J. C. Rogers was astounded by the absurd formality of a messenger from General Law. Said the aide: "General Law presents his compliments, and says hold this place at all hazard."

"Compliments hell!" bellowed Rogers. "Who wants compliments in such a damned place as this? Go back and ask General Law if he expects me to hold the whole world with the 5th Texas Regiment."

Hobart Ward's brigade grudgingly gives ground as Hood's Confederate attackers scramble through the Devil's Den. Ward lost more than a third of his men but inflicted heavy losses on Hood's troops. Wrote one Texan, "Both sides were whipped and all were mad about it."

On the rocky crest above the Devil's Den, the 1st Texas and 15th Georgia closed in on James Smith's 4th New York Battery. With his supply of canister nearly exhausted, the captain shouted to his gunners, "Give them shell! Give them solid shot! Damn them, give them anything!" A single salvo cut down 15 Texans, but despite the gaps torn in their ranks, the Confederates came on, screaming the Rebel yell. With tears in his eyes, Smith implored his infantry's support, "For God's sake, men, don't let them take my guns away from me!"

Striving desperately to protect Smith's guns, Major James Cromwell of the Orange Blossoms rode to the front of the line and led a charge that dislodged the Confederates. He shouted, "The day is ours!" In an instant, he was struck by a bullet and fell dead from his saddle. The Confederates surged back. The redoubtable Augustus Van Horne Ellis then mounted a countercharge, crying, "My God! My God, men! Your major's down; save him! Save him!" Seeing the Southerners reel, Ellis stood in his stirrups and flourished his sword. At that moment a bullet slammed into his forehead, and he pitched dead among the rocks.

In the ensuing melee, men in blue and gray found themselves on opposite sides of the same boulder, reaching around its circumference to fire muzzle to muzzle; others used their bayonets to stab blindly around the corners of crevices. The struggle, recalled a Confederate, was "more like Indian fighting than anything I experienced during the war." When at last the engagement sputtered to an end, the Confederates had possession of the Devil's Den and the ridge above, along with three of Smith's guns. The de-

Augustus Van Horne Ellis, colonel of the 124th New York, had led a full life before he fell at Gettysburg. A New York City lawyer, he ventured to California, becoming a fireman and then a sailor. Voyaging to Hawaii, he made friends with the islands' king and was appointed commander of Hawaii's navy. When he learned that the king had no warships, Ellis returned home to become a steamer captain.

fending Federals of Ward's 2,200-man brigade had suffered 781 casualties.

The fight on the south flank had been, at its most intense, a struggle of private soldiers acting on their own instincts. Private Val Giles of the 4th Texas wrote later of the contest on Little Round Top, "Every fellow was his own general. Private soldiers gave commands as loud as the officers; nobody paying any attention to either." To the north, around the Peach Orchard, another stage of this chaotic soldier's battle was erupting.

An Artist's Portrayal of the Battle

Among the most dramatic and accurate paintings of the Battle of Gettysburg are those by a Pennsylvania-born artist named Peter Frederick Rothermel. Commissioned by the Pennsylvania state legislature in 1866 to portray the great battle, Rothermel, an experienced historical artist, threw himself with ardor into the task, studying his subject for four years before putting brush to canvas. He tramped the fields around Gettysburg with soldiers who had fought there and with civilians who knew the terrain. He traveled thousands of miles to visit veterans, transcribing their first-hand accounts and sketching their faces. He corresponded with many of the generals involved in the battle.

When Rothermel at last unlimbered his paints and brushes in 1870, he executed not just one painting, as he had been commissioned to do, but rather a series of canvases, five of which are shown here and on the following pages. Each canvas depicts a critical moment in the three days of furious fighting. The masterpiece of the series, a portrayal of Pickett's Charge (*pages 96-97*), filled a stupendous canvas, 16¾ by 32 feet in size; it remains one of the largest framed paintings in the world. Thanks to Rothermel's exhaustive research, the works are remarkably accurate; they depict the Battle of Gettysburg as it actually was — a grim struggle between two armies of uncommonly brave common soldiers.

Rothermel's painting of action on the battle's first day, July 1, shows litter-bearers (*center foreground*) carrying off the body of Union General John Reynolds. In the

background, troops of Reynolds' I Corps try to blunt the assault of General Henry Heth's Confederates, who push across McPherson's Farm toward Gettysburg.

On July 2, General Samuel Crawford's Pennsylvania Reserve Division charges into Plum Run Valley, through ...al Confederate of Longstreet's co...

The 5th Maine Battery *(foreground)*, anchoring the Union defenses on Cemetery Hill, fires into the left flank of General Harry Hays's Louisiana Tigers during a

Confederate assault at dusk on July 2. At far left, Colonel Samuel Carroll's brigade of the Union II Corps countercharges head-on into the advancing Louisianians.

thermel's painting of the Confederate attack... Culp's Hill... the morning of July 3 as seen by...

the charging regiment. The Federal defenders *(foreground and right)* repulsed the assault; the dog was killed, along with 31 men of the 1st Maryland.

Rothermel's huge work depicting the moment when Federal forces (*left*) repulsed Pickett's Charge centers on a heroic private of the 72nd Pennsylvania, who stands

coatless, wielding his musket as a club; an impassive General Meade observes the action from his horse at far left.

Fury in the Peach Orchard

"The struggle was almost hand-to-hand. There was no wavering or shadow of turning; it seemed as if the last man would there find his allotted ounce of lead."

CAPTAIN GEORGE W. VERRILL, 17TH MAINE, IN THE WHEAT FIELD

On the morning of July 2, while visiting Ewell's front, General Lee had made an observation filled with foreboding. "The enemy have the advantage of us in a shorter and inside line," he said, "and we are too extended." Later calculations would confirm his point. From the Federal right near Culp's Hill to the left on Little Round Top, Meade's hook-shaped line stretched three miles — and he had available an average of 17,000 infantrymen per mile. Arrayed outside that arc, the Confederate army formed a line two miles longer and proportionately thinner, averaging only 10,000 men per mile.

Moreover, the Federal troops could move quickly from one place to another on their line simply by cutting across the arc. For example, moving an infantry regiment from the XII Corps position on Culp's Hill to the Federal center, a mile away on Cemetery Ridge, would take no more than 20 minutes at the double-quick. In no case was the marching distance between two Federal positions more than two and a half miles.

In the fighting that followed the Confederate assaults on Little Round Top and the Devil's Den, General Meade would use his advantage to the fullest, borrowing from quiet parts of his front to patch his line where it was in danger. His efforts would be aided not only by the topography but by the unevenness of the Confederate attack.

As planned, Lee's echelon attack would begin in the south and move gradually northward along Cemetery Ridge; but it would not proceed, as Lee had hoped, in an orderly, overpowering succession of triphammer blows. The failure of his commands to advance at exactly the right moment would cause breakdowns in the carefully contrived sequence of the assault. Thus Lee's attack unfolded in fits and starts, sputtering, now fierce and now feeble. The battle quickly slid out of control for the Confederates, and in time Lee's plan would dissolve in confusion.

While their comrades had been storming Little Round Top and the Devil's Den, Confederates on Hood's left — General George Anderson's brigade, along with some of Henry Benning's men — had been butting up against David Birney's thin but obstinate line along the ridge running from the Devil's Den northwest to the Peach Orchard. If the Confederates could penetrate Birney's line, they would find themselves within the Federal salient — and in the rear of Sickles' right wing, which stretched from the orchard northeastward along the Emmitsburg road.

Although Anderson's veteran Georgians had few peers as assault troops, they made little headway against Birney; Anderson himself was among the wounded. Clearly, they needed help, and McLaws' division — poised just to the north — was growing increasingly restless under the restraints imposed by Longstreet, the corps commander. Hood's onslaught had passed its fullest fury before Longstreet finally sent McLaws into battle at about 5:30 p.m.

The brigade on McLaws' right, which according to Lee's echelon plan would strike first, was commanded by Brigadier General Joseph B. Kershaw, a South Carolina lawyer and politician who fought as if born to the blare of bugles. Longstreet accompanied Kershaw on foot as far as the Emmitsburg road, then sent him forward with a shout and a wave of his hat.

Crossing the Emmitsburg road, three of Kershaw's South Carolina regiments wheeled north in a vain attempt to breach the Federal line in the Peach Orchard. The remaining two leaped a stone fence and charged eastward to join Anderson's Confederates near what would soon be known simply as the Wheat Field. As the two regiments advanced across the property of a farmer named John P. Rose, they were swept by a flailing fire. One of Kershaw's men recalled the canister that raked his line: "Oh the awful, deathly swishing sounds of those little black balls as they flew by us, through us, between our legs and over us."

The brunt of the Confederate attack near the Wheat Field fell on a small brigade under Colonel Régis de Trobriand, an aristocratic French lawyer, poet and author — but above all, a passionate soldier. As de Trobriand rode up and down his line, shouting encouragement in heavily accented English, his troops held out against the worst that Anderson and Kershaw could deliver. A Georgia brigade under Brigadier General Paul J. Semmes — brother of the famed Confederate commerce raider Raphael Semmes — followed Kershaw, adding its weight to the assault. As he was bringing his men up, Semmes fell with a wound in the thigh; he would later die. Confused, his Georgians wavered and lost momentum, but the

brigade soon rallied and came on again.

Suddenly there was disaster to the right of de Trobriand. The line between his troops and the Peach Orchard was held by a V Corps division under 62-year-old Brigadier General James Barnes. Many of Barnes's troops were firing from behind a stone wall that offered substantial protection. An officer in Barnes's division believed his troops could hold their favorable position "against considerable odds 'till the cows come." They might have, too, had not the cautious General Barnes ordered a withdrawal, leaving a huge gap in the Federal line.

With his right flank exposed, de Trobriand was also forced to pull back, suffering heavy casualties along the way. The Confederates streamed across the Wheat Field, whooping in exultation, only to collide head-on with fresh Federal troops who came in on

the double, firing as they charged. These desperately needed reinforcements were the men of Brigadier General John C. Caldwell's division, which had been shifted from the left flank of II Corps on Cemetery Ridge. General Hancock had dispatched the division to Sickles' aid at 5:15 p.m. despite the fact that he was thus widening the dangerous gap between II Corps and III Corps.

Caldwell had no time to indulge in elaborate tactics; he simply fed his brigades into the fray as they arrived at the Wheat Field. First to appear was a brigade under Colonel Edward E. Cross, a salty old Indian fighter who went into battle with a black silk handkerchief tied around his bald head. Earlier, as Cross's brigade was leaving Cemetery Ridge, General Hancock had called to its commander, hinting at a promotion to come: "Cross, this is the last time you'll fight with-

With one dead and one wounded soldier sprawled at his feet, Father William Corby stands on a boulder to give absolution to kneeling troops of the Irish Brigade about to go into battle. Wrote a Pennsylvania soldier who witnessed the ceremony: "No doubt many a prayer from men of Protestant faith who could conscientiously not bow the knee went up to God in that impressive moment."

out a star!" Without so much as pausing, Cross replied over his shoulder: "Too late, general. This is my last battle."

Ten minutes later, in the woods at the Wheat Field's southern edge, Cross was fatally wounded. He died that night, murmuring: "I think the boys will miss me."

Cross's brigade was followed by that of Brigadier General Samuel K. Zook, who found his way barred by Barnes's retreating troops. The fiery Zook was enraged. "If you can't get out of the way," he roared, "lie down and we will march over you." In an extraordinary scene, Barnes's men did indeed lie down, and over their prone bodies Zook's brigade plunged into the Wheat Field. Zook was among the first to fall. As he leaped his horse over a stone wall into the Wheat Field, he was shot in the stomach and mortally wounded.

To the right of Cross's troops, marched the 532 men of Colonel Patrick Kelly's Irish Brigade, the emerald green of its harp-bedecked flag now faded from long, hard use. On being ordered to the Wheat Field, the Irishmen had participated in a ceremony that one officer called "awe-inspiring." With the thunder of battle serving as his accompaniment, Father William Corby, the brigade chaplain, had mounted a rock and pronounced upon the kneeling men and officers the general absolution — *"Dominus noster Jesus Christus vos absolvat."* Father Corby was careful to add, however, that "the Catholic Church refuses Christian burial to the soldier who turns his back upon the foe." Advancing into the trampled, corpse-strewn field, the Irishmen plugged the gap between Cross's troops and Zook's and started shooting. "The effect of our fire was deadly in the extreme," recalled Major St. Clair Mulhol-

Brigadier General Cadmus Marcellus Wilcox, whose brigade of Alabamians nearly breached the Federal line at Cemetery Ridge, was a cool professional soldier more noted for his reliability than his brilliance. Lee valued him as an old-line Army man who was "properly assignable anywhere."

land of the 116th Pennsylvania. "A blind man could not have missed his mark."

Finally, Caldwell threw in his last brigade, under 24-year-old Colonel John Brooke. Caldwell would later be criticized for his piecemeal tactics; unlike many commanders at Gettysburg, however, he at least got all his men into the battle. Brooke led a magnificent charge, and Semmes's Georgians slowed, stopped and began giving ground.

But not for long. Rallying at the Rose farm, back they rushed, reinforced by another Georgia brigade, under Brigadier General William T. Wofford, who brought his men down on Caldwell's right flank. For the sixth time the Wheat Field changed hands. Briefly, knots of Federals stood their ground, grappling hand to hand with the Georgians. One Confederate seized the flag of the 4th Michigan but was shot dead by the regiment's commander, Colonel Harrison Jeffords. As Jeffords snatched up the fallen banner, he was run through by a Confederate bayonet and killed. At last, with the help of a fresh V Corps division, the Federals were able to restore Birney's line between the Wheat Field and the Devil's Den.

Preoccupied with the assault against their left, however, Sickles and Meade had either ignored, or been ignorant of, the menace to the Peach Orchard. Even as the fighting raged in the Wheat Field, the Confederates on McLaws' left had launched an attack from the woods west of the orchard. Leading that assault was Brigadier General William Barksdale, whose Mississippi brigade was scheduled to advance next in echelon after Kershaw and Semmes. Barksdale had been frantic to get going; a barrel-chested former U.S. Congressman, he had what one of his men called "a thirst for battle glory." The

enemy was just a tantalizing 600 yards away, and Barksdale's aggressive inclinations were being severely aggravated by a Union battery in the Peach Orchard that was pounding away at his waiting men.

"General," he begged McLaws, "let me charge." And again: "General, let me go." McLaws was, of course, helpless until Longstreet gave the word; and when finally Longstreet rode past, Barksdale pleaded with him: "I wish you would let me go in, General; I will take that battery in five minutes."

"Wait a little," replied Longstreet. "We are all going in presently." By the time Longstreet finally judged the time to be right, he had received a bonus: The Federals defending the Wheat Field had been so battered by the fighting that they would be unable to support Sickles' isolated corps. At that opportune moment—around 6:30 p.m.—Longstreet at last let Barksdale go.

Drums began to roll, and Barksdale rode to the front of his old regiment, the 13th Mississippi, to take his place before its flag. As he turned toward the enemy, an aide saw that his face was "radiant with joy." Barksdale gave a simple command and repeated it time and again while riding toward the enemy: "Forward, men, forward!"

From 1,600 throats came the Rebel yell, and out of the covering timber burst the Mississippians. "At top speed," recalled one of them, "without firing a shot, the brigade sped swiftly across the field and literally rushed the goal." A Federal colonel recalled the enemy's lunge as "the grandest charge that was ever made by mortal man." The gray tide bore down on the apex of the Peach Orchard salient, which was held by Brigadier General Charles K. Graham's men.

The Confederates smashed down the rail fences along both sides of the road and were through the Federal line and into the Peach Orchard in even less time than the five minutes Barksdale had estimated. Covered by their infantry support, the Federal batteries began pulling back. Two of the regiments in Graham's brigade—the 57th and the 114th Pennsylvania—ventured across the Emmitsburg road to cover the withdrawal of one of the batteries. They had barely taken position beside the Sherfy farmhouse when Confederate volleys swept them aside. Some wounded men who crawled into the Sherfy barn perished when the building burst into flames. Graham was also wounded; he fought on until his horse fell and threw him heavily to the ground. Then, dazed and bleeding, he was taken prisoner. In minutes the brigade had lost 740 of its 1,516 men.

In the same attack, the III Corps would lose its commander. On horseback near his Trostle farm headquarters, about a quarter mile north of the Wheat Field, Sickles was

At the tip of the Peach Orchard salient, Union General Daniel Sickles spurs ahead of his staff to inspect the front lines of his threatened III Corps on the afternoon of July 2. Confederates can be seen massing for an attack by the fringe of trees in the distance.

hit by a solid shot that left his right leg dangling below the knee by a few shreds of flesh. As aides helped him from his horse, Sickles calmly directed a drummer boy who was acting as a litter-bearer to apply a tourniquet to his leg. Sickles then ordered his command turned over to Birney, and to counter a swiftly spreading rumor that he was dead, he lit up a big Havana cigar and puffed it ostentatiously while being carried to the rear. He lost the leg but lived to conduct a lifelong feud with Meade over the efficacy of the III Corps advance to the Peach Orchard.

The III Corps line was finally broken. The rout of Graham's division in the salient now exposed the flank of Caldwell's forces down by the Wheat Field, enabling Wofford's Georgians to push the Federals back there.

Long after the War, Robert H. Carter of the 22nd Massachusetts vividly remembered the scene of chaos as the Federal lines at the Wheat Field and the Peach Orchard gave way before Longstreet's attack. "The hoarse

and indistinguishable orders of commanding officers, the screaming and bursting of shells, canister and shrapnel as they tore through the struggling masses of humanity, the death screams of wounded animals, the groans of their human companions, wounded and dying and trampled under foot by hurrying batteries, riderless horses and the moving lines of battle, all combined an indescribable roar of discordant elements — in fact a perfect hell on earth, never, perhaps to be equaled, certainly not to be surpassed, nor *ever* to be forgotten in a man's lifetime. It has never been effaced from my memory, day or night, for fifty years."

From the II Corps lines on Cemetery Ridge, Lieutenant Frank A. Haskell, an aide to Brigadier General John Gibbon, despairingly watched the Confederate onslaught. "The Third Corps is being overpowered," Haskell would remember later. "Here and there its lines begin to break — the men begin to pour back to the rear in confusion — the enemy are upon them and among them. Organization is lost to a great degree. Guns and caissons are abandoned and in the hands of the enemy. The Third Corps, after a heroic but unfortunate fight, is being literally swept from the field."

Had Haskell looked closer, he would have seen that part of III Corps — the division commanded by Brigadier General Andrew A. Humphreys along the salient's north leg — was retiring in good order, fighting fiercely as it went. Humphreys, a lean professional soldier, was in a towering temper.

To begin with, Humphreys had not liked the position in which Sickles had placed his division — way out in front of the rest of the army and stretched for three quarters of a mile along the Emmitsburg road with its right flank exposed. Then Sickles had sent Humphreys' Excelsior Brigade to support Graham's line in the Peach Orchard and had also diverted a V Corps brigade that had been on its way to reinforce Humphreys. Referring to Sickles' penchant for shuffling troops around, Humphreys fumed: "This ruinous habit is disgusting."

With the collapse of Birney's line, Humphreys' left flank was also exposed. At that point, he pulled back part of his division in hopes of linking up with Birney's right wing, but found "nobody to form the new line but myself— Birney's troops cleared out."

Moreover, Humphreys was by now under fierce attack from fresh Confederate brigades. With the unleashing of Barksdale and Wofford, Longstreet had put all the available units of his corps into action, and responsibility for continuing the echelon sequence now passed to A. P. Hill's corps— specifically, to the division commanded by Brigadier General Richard H. Anderson.

Although Anderson's career had been marked by strange interludes of indolence, he could fight well enough when he felt like it, and it looked as if this was going to be one of his good days; he got his right into action shortly after Barksdale swept over the Peach Orchard. Attacking in rapid succession across the Emmitsburg road, the brigades under the reliable Brigadier General Cadmus Wilcox and Colonel David Lang slammed into Humphreys' isolated line at about the same time, overlapping it on both flanks and shoving it back toward Cemetery Ridge.

Humphreys, however, managed to keep his troops more or less in hand, riding up and down his ragged line, steadying the men. Though his horse was wounded six times, it somehow stayed on its feet — and the general

remained on its back. Then, hit by a seventh bullet, the horse reared and threw Humphreys to the ground; he borrowed an aide's horse and quickly went back to work.

"Twenty times," Humphreys recalled, "did I bring my men to a halt and face about." At last he got the survivors to the crest of Cemetery Ridge, where Hancock placed them on the left of II Corps — to fill at least part of the hole left earlier by the departure of Caldwell's division. Their number, as Hancock recalled it, "was very small, scarcely equal to an ordinary battalion." Humphreys had lost more than 2,000 of his 5,000 men on the fields between the Emmitsburg road and Cemetery Ridge. In one regiment, the 120th New York, 17 officers had fallen.

And still the Confederate blows continued. Now two more of Anderson's brigades attacked, north of Humphreys' former position. The 1,413 Confederates under Brigadier General Ambrose R. Wright made dramatic progress; the memory was still fresh when Wright wrote five days later to his wife: "We worked our way across that terrible field for more than a mile, under the most furious fire of artillery that I had ever seen." At the Emmitsburg road Wright's men came up against two Federal regiments posted near the Codori farmhouse and barn. Wright swept this opposition aside, then paused before pressing his attack on Cemetery Ridge.

Looking westward from Cemetery Ridge, one II Corps officer saw the Confederates coming "like the fury of a whirlwind." Wrote another: "The whole slope in our front is full of them; and in various formation, in line, in column, and in masses which are neither, with yells and thick volleys they are rushing toward our crest."

The Federal left and center were in mortal

danger. But the stubborn resistance in the Wheat Field and on Humphreys' front had gained for the Federal commanders what they needed most — the time to rush reinforcements from the quiet side of their hook-shaped line.

General Meade sent two additional V Corps brigades to consolidate the shaky position on Little Round Top. Dispatched from

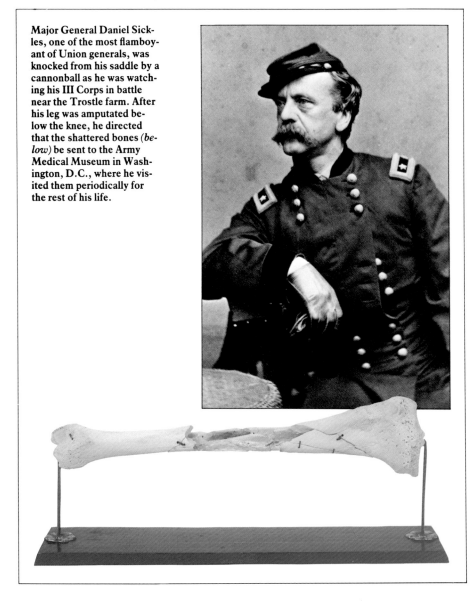

Major General Daniel Sickles, one of the most flamboyant of Union generals, was knocked from his saddle by a cannonball as he was watching his III Corps in battle near the Trostle farm. After his leg was amputated below the knee, he directed that the shattered bones (*below*) be sent to the Army Medical Museum in Washington, D.C., where he visited them periodically for the rest of his life.

Culp's Hill, most of XII Corps rushed cross-country toward the sound of the guns. The I Corps divisions of Abner Doubleday and John Robinson, weakened by the battering they had taken the previous day, nonetheless hastened to respond from their position behind Cemetery Hill. And out of reserve came three of Sedgwick's VI Corps brigades, exhausted by their marathon overnight march.

Meanwhile, between the Peach Orchard and Cemetery Ridge, artillery chief Henry Hunt was scrounging for guns to defend an improvised line on a low rise just east of Plum Run. And as the Confederate attack began to develop, General Hancock was skillfully juggling his II Corps units to strengthen his Cemetery Ridge line.

Thus, as the Confederate brigades trotted across the fields south of Gettysburg and flung themselves at the enemy, they were time and again confronted by reinforcements that had arrived only moments before. The Confederates who had broken through at the Wheat Field, for example, pursued the Federal survivors toward Little Round Top. Later, one Confederate would claim that "nothing but the exhausted condition of the men prevented them from carrying the heights." But in fact it was V Corps troops — the Pennsylvania Reserve Division under Brigadier General Samuel W. Crawford — who turned the tide, charging down the hill and driving the Confederates back to the Wheat Field.

To the north, Barksdale's assault had also run into trouble. After sweeping across the Peach Orchard, Barksdale veered slightly to his left. Waving his sword and still shouting his men forward, he led his brigade toward the Trostle house and barn. There, the Mississippians met surprisingly stiff opposition from some gallant Federal artillerymen.

In their fighting retreat from the Peach Orchard, four Federal batteries had lost so many horses that some of their cannon had to be hauled off by hand. The batteries, commanded by Lieutenant Colonel Freeman McGilvery of Maine, paused near the Trostle barn and briefly checked the advance of the 21st Mississippi, one of Barksdale's regiments. Then, under pressure on his front and both flanks, McGilvery again hauled his guns back — this time to the rise east of Plum Run — leaving at Trostle's farm a Massachusetts battery of six 12-pounders under Captain John Bigelow.

McGilvery next rode to the crest of Cemetery Ridge, expecting to find infantry to support his guns. Instead, there were only some wild-eyed survivors of III Corps, who kept right on going across the ridge in search of refuge to the east. Looking back, McGilvery saw that Bigelow was preparing to withdraw before being overrun by Barksdale's brigade; there would be no way to stop the Confederates from punching straight through the main Federal line on Cemetery Ridge.

Without a moment's hesitation, McGilvery dug his spurs into his horse's flanks and galloped through a storm of shot and shell toward Bigelow; struck by several bullets, the horse lurched, recovered and made it to Bigelow's position. McGilvery instructed Bigelow to hold on at all cost until a stronger artillery line could be formed on the little ridge beyond Plum Run.

Firing round after round of deadly canister, Bigelow's cannoneers managed to slow Barksdale's charge for a few minutes. Then the 21st Mississippi swept down on the battery's right flank. Having lost 28 men, four guns and most of his horses, Bigelow, bleed-

Dead artillery horses litter the yard of the Trostle house, where the guns of Captain John Bigelow's 9th Massachusetts Battery delayed the charging 21st Mississippi for precious minutes while a second Federal defensive line was formed. Bigelow recalled that the Confederates climbed atop his limber chests, "yelling like demons," to fire at the gunners.

ing profusely from two wounds, led a withdrawal. During those priceless moments of resistance, McGilvery had rounded up several more batteries and placed them along what would henceforth be known as the Plum Run line. His prospects were decidedly dim; field artillery without infantry support could not for long withstand the determined assault of Barksdale and his Mississippians.

McGilvery opened fire. "Our batteries plowed lanes through the living masses in front of them," one Federal recalled. But the Confederates kept coming, overrunning Battery I of the 5th U.S. Artillery. Now McGilvery was attracting shells from Colonel E. Porter Alexander's Confederate gunners, who had unlimbered in the Peach Orchard. Soon the Federals were down to a dozen operable guns, then six, and the end seemed close at hand.

At 7:15 p.m., Federal reinforcements arrived. Colonel George C. Burling's brigade, detached from Humphreys' command, reached the Plum Run line and formed in support of McGilvery's guns. In addition, down from the northern end of the II Corps position on Cemetery Ridge came Colonel George L. Willard's brigade of General Alexander Hays's division.

Willard's brigade, led by General Hancock himself, charged down the slope of the ridge, crashed through the elderberry thickets that lined the stream and struck the center of Barksdale's brigade. Willard went down in the assault, decapitated by a shell. But the Confederates were badly shaken and slowly began to fall back.

Barksdale, who was by one account "almost frantic with rage," strove to rally his Mississippians. Then he too was shot from the saddle. According to Gettysburg legend,

a Federal officer ordered an entire company to fire at the inspirational Confederate commander. True or not, Barksdale's chest and legs were riddled with bullets. He died of his wounds that night, after gasping to a Federal surgeon, "Tell my wife I am shot, but we fought like hell."

So far, units of III Corps and II Corps had opposed Barksdale's brigade — and now it was the turn of XII Corps. Earlier, Major

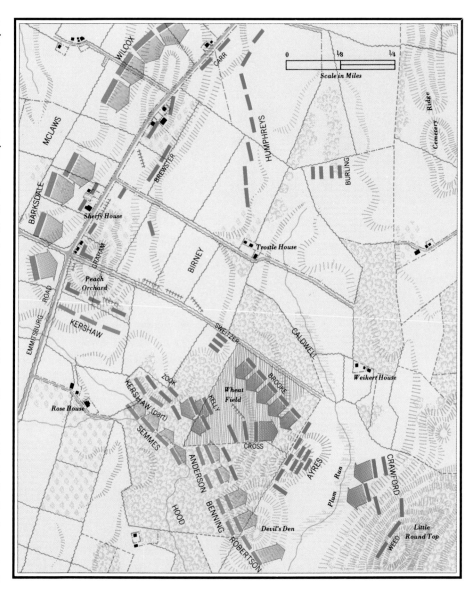

At 5:30 p.m. on July 2, Lafayette McLaws' Confederate division attacked the salient held by Daniel Sickles' III Corps. The Wheat Field changed hands six times as Confederate brigades led by Joseph Kershaw, Paul Semmes and George T. Anderson were counterattacked by the four brigades of John Caldwell's II Corps division. At 6:30 p.m., McLaws launched William Barksdale's brigade in a charge that swept through the Peach Orchard and shattered the Federal salient.

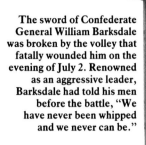

The sword of Confederate General William Barksdale was broken by the volley that fatally wounded him on the evening of July 2. Renowned as an aggressive leader, Barksdale had told his men before the battle, "We have never been whipped and we never can be."

General Alpheus S. Williams, who was in temporary command of the corps while Slocum supervised the army's right wing, had been instructed by Meade to move his men over from Culp's Hill. But no one told General Williams precisely where to go, and no guide was provided.

Williams simply headed for the spot where he heard the most noise. After a while, as he wrote later, he picked up a trail of debris left by men fleeing the battlefield — "broken gun-carriages, scattered arms, knapsacks, blankets and clothing of all kinds." Soon McGilvery rode up in frantic search of help. He was, as Williams laconically described the meeting, "delighted to see me." Though McGilvery did not know it, Barksdale's brigade was by now on its last legs, and only one of Williams' regiments would be required to finish the job. "It met little resistance," Williams wrote, "for the Rebs ran."

Even as Barksdale's men broke for the rear, however, General Hancock saw trouble to the north: Cadmus Wilcox's Confederate brigade was heading straight for the gap on Cemetery Ridge that had been left when Caldwell's division departed for the Wheat Field. Hancock ordered Gibbon and Hays to send help from their divisions, but there was no way the men could get there before Wilcox did. As Hancock subsequently recalled his plight, "In some way five minutes must be gained or we were lost."

He was granted his five minutes, and a few more, by a small regiment that stood in line of battle on Cemetery Ridge behind an artillery battery. Galloping toward them, Hancock called out: "What regiment is this?" Colonel William Colvill shouted back that it was the 1st Minnesota, which had been detached earlier that day from the rest of Gibbon's division. "Colonel, do you see those colors?" asked Hancock, pointing to the Confederate battle flag in the front rank of Wilcox's brigade. Colvill nodded. "Then take them," Hancock ordered. As Lieutenant William Lochren of the 1st Minnesota recalled, "Every man realized in an instant what that order meant — death or wounds to us all, the sacrifice of the regiment to gain a few minutes' time and save the position."

And so they charged, one undersized regiment against an entire brigade, down the ridge with muskets at a right shoulder shift, their bayonets flashing. Just before they reached the Confederate lines, Colvill shouted, "Charge bayonets," and the muskets were lowered, presenting a solid front of steel. Wrote Lochren: "The men were never made who will stand against leveled bayonets coming with such momentum and evident desperation. The ferocity of our onset seemed to paralyze them for a time." The Confederate line crumbled.

Before the Confederates could recover from the shock of the mad countercharge, other regiments from Gibbon's division had filled the void on Cemetery Ridge and were pouring a withering fire into Wilcox's men. Of the 262 Minnesotans who had so fearlessly hurled themselves at Wilcox's brigade, only 47 men remained fit for combat. This toll, 82 per cent of those engaged, was the highest of any Union regiment in the War.

Stalled, Wilcox sent a plea for reinforcements to his division commander, Richard Anderson. After his brisk beginning, Anderson had failed to keep up with the battle. The courier from Wilcox found him in the woods on Seminary Ridge, chatting with staff officers and paying slight attention to the murderous fight in which his di-

vision was engaged. When informed of Wilcox's urgent need, Anderson replied almost casually: "Tell General Wilcox to hold his own, that things will change."

Without help from Anderson, Wilcox had no choice but to withdraw as best he could. Gibbon's Federal troops pursued him and also swarmed around David Lang's little Florida brigade, halted in a stand of trees to Wilcox's left. At that point Lang wisely decided to get out while the getting was good. The withdrawals left Anderson's northernmost brigade on the field — the Georgians under Ambrose Wright — all alone, a mile in front of the rest of Lee's army.

Nearing the top of Cemetery Ridge, Wright's brigade came to a place where two stone walls joined at a right angle. Crouching behind them, the Georgians fired on some Federal batteries, then leaped over the walls and drove off the cannoneers with bayonets and musket butts. Wright thought he had pierced the Federal center. "We were now complete masters of the field," he wrote later, "having gained the key to the enemy's whole line." In fact, Wright was still quite a few yards short of the crest of Cemetery Ridge, and just over it on the opposite slope, sheltered from the fire of Confederate guns, was the so-called Philadelphia Brigade of Gibbon's division.

This veteran unit had fallen on sad times and had become known for its slack discipline as the "Straggler Brigade." Just a few days earlier, it had been taken over by a 28-year-old, spit-and-polish career soldier named Alexander Webb. Wearing his fresh brigadier's stars, Webb had cracked down hard, berating officers for their slovenly appearance and promising to personally shoot stragglers "like dogs." The men grumbled

111

and hissed their new commander but knew he meant business—and when he ordered them to charge over the ridge top and drive Wright from his lodgement, they obeyed.

Just then, in what had become the firmly established pattern of the day, Federal reinforcements arrived—Doubleday's I Corps division, followed closely by Robinson's. While Webb's men hit Wright from the front, the others began working around his flanks and to his rear. "We were about to be sacrificed to the bad management and cowardly conduct of others," Wright said later, embittered because he had received no help from Confederates on his right and left. "With cheers and good order we turned our faces to the enemy in our rear, and abandoning our captured guns we rushed upon the flanking column of the enemy and literally cut our way out."

The Confederate troops that were to have attacked on Wright's left—a brigade under Brigadier General Carnot Posey—had stalled completely. Even before reaching the Emmitsburg road, Posey's men had run into Federal skirmishers who had decided to stand fast. From his position on Cemetery Hill, General Hays saw the little fight developing far out on his front and sent five companies to help the skirmishers. That was enough for Posey, who made no attempt to go farther.

On Posey's left, Brigadier General William Mahone took his cue from Posey and stayed put. Toward the end of the War, the wispy, cold-eyed little Mahone would become one of Lee's most dependable division commanders. But on this day he flatly refused to advance his brigade, insisting, "I have my orders from General Anderson himself to stay here." Even when Anderson

roused himself enough to send orders to attack, Mahone remained adamantly inactive.

The aggressive young General William Dorsey Pender rode over from the left of Mahone to find out the cause of the delay. Pender, whose division was next in line to attack, undoubtedly would have ordered his men forward with or without Mahone, but on the way he was struck in the leg by a shell fragment. The wound did not appear to be fatal, but it forced him from the field; several days later, the leg would have to be amputated, and Pender would die a few hours after the operation.

With two divisions thus stalled, Lee's

Fighting from the cover of boulders and tree trunks, Confederates of Colonel J. M. Williams' 14th and 15th Louisiana push their way up Culp's Hill against the 60th and 102nd New York, whose breastworks are visible at the crest. The advance of the Louisianians started in twilight and continued in complete darkness. "We had but the flashes of their guns to guide our fire," recalled a Confederate officer.

Major General William Dorsey Pender was so highly valued for his aggressiveness that Lee believed he would have won at Gettysburg if Pender had not been mortally wounded before ordering his division into battle. One of Pender's officers called him "one of the coolest, most self-possessed and absolutely fearless men under fire I ever knew."

echelon sequence broke down completely around 8 p.m. Lee wrote afterward of his belief that "if General Pender had remained on his horse half an hour longer we would have carried the enemy's position." But there were other, more basic reasons for the failure of the Confederate attack on Gettysburg's second day.

Among other things, several commanding officers — including Anderson, A. P. Hill and Lee himself — had been little more than spectators during the complicated attack. One observer later reported that Lee had sent only one dispatch, and received only one, during the entire afternoon. Beyond that, Lee's verbal orders had evidently been fuzzy: For example, General A. P. Hill seemed to think that Richard Anderson's division had been detached from his corps to Longstreet's, while Longstreet assumed that it remained in Hill's command. Because of such confusion, a member of Lee's staff said later, "the whole affair was disjointed. There was an utter absence of accord in the movements of the several commands."

Even more important, General Ewell, on the extreme left, had frittered away the afternoon hours that might have won the day for the Confederacy.

By midmorning, most of Ewell's troops had been in place and ready to accomplish their primary mission — to pin down the Federal forces on Culp's and Cemetery Hills and prevent them from going to the aid of Federal units being attacked by Longstreet and Hill. On Ewell's left, Edward Johnson's division was deployed about a mile northeast of Culp's Hill. In the center, Jubal Early's division was hidden behind a rise that stretched east of Gettysburg, about a half mile from Cemetery Hill. On the right, Robert Rodes's division was entangled in the streets of Gettysburg and would have to move out of town to the west before it could have a clear shot at Cemetery Hill from the northwest.

As General Ewell waited for the sound of guns from the Confederate right, he did nothing to prepare beyond tinkering with his artillery emplacements. He did not discuss with Johnson, Early or Rodes how they should cooperate in the demonstration.

Meanwhile, the men waited, restless and chafing in the hot sun. "Greatly did the officers and men marvel," recalled an officer of Johnson's division, "as morning, noon and

afternoon passed in inaction—on our part, not on the enemy's, for, as we well know, he was plying axe and pick and shovel in fortifying a position which was already sufficiently formidable."

Indeed, the forces of the Federal right— Howard's XI Corps on Cemetery Hill, and Slocum's XII Corps along with Wadsworth's sadly depleted I Corps division on Culp's Hill—were digging in with all the urgency of men who had learned the hard way about the striking power of Confederate infantry. Nowhere was the work carried out more effectively than on the left of the XII Corps line, which was held by Brigadier General George Sears Greene.

The 62-year-old general had the gaunt and burning visage of an Old Testament prophet. He was, in the words of one of his officers, "a grim old fighter." But Greene was more than that: After graduating second in his class at West Point, he had taught engineering at the academy, then resigned from the Army to become one of the leading civil engineers in the East. Greene was expert at building field fortifications, and by late afternoon his brigade had erected breastworks of earth and heavy logs that were five feet high.

Perhaps because of some unusual atmospheric condition that day, Ewell apparently did not hear Longstreet's opening bombardment and for some time afterward did nothing. When at length he did stir, it was not with an infantry demonstration but with an artillery barrage. For more than two hours, while Longstreet's and Hill's divisions were battering themselves into bloody exhaustion, Ewell's guns atop Benner's Hill, half a mile northeast of the Federal position, banged fruitlessly away at the enemy emplacements on Cemetery and Culp's Hills.

The better situated and more accurate Federal batteries answered in kind; slowly, relentlessly, the Federal metal wore down Ewell's batteries, demolishing guns, exploding limber chests and fatally wounding Ewell's 20-year-old artillery commander, Major J. W. Latimer. At about 6:30 p.m.

These unidentified Confederate infantrymen belonged to General Harry Hays's Louisiana Tiger Brigade, which swarmed over Ricketts' battery on Cemetery Hill. Mostly French-speaking Creoles, the Louisianians were "the best marchers in the army and gay and grand in battle," according to an admiring South Carolinian who saw them in action.

Attack of the Louisiana Tigers on a battery of the 11th Corps

Against heavy fire, troops of the 9th Louisiana charge Ricketts' Pennsylvania battery on the crest of Cemetery Hill after nightfall on July 2. "The enemy stood with a tenacity never before displayed by them," recalled a Confederate officer, "but with bayonet, clubbed musket, sword and pistol, and rocks from the wall, we cleared the heights and silenced the guns."

the Confederate gunners were forced to withdraw out of range.

At that inauspicious moment, without the slightest notion of what was happening on the Confederate right, Ewell decided to launch a full-scale infantry attack. By that time he had already failed to do what Lee had asked of him; most of the Federal forces on Culp's Hill and roughly half of the units on Cemetery Hill had gone to bolster the line against Longstreet and Hill.

Although Ewell issued no written orders, he evidently meant to attack progressively from his left to his right. Johnson's division — more than 5,000 strong — moved first, toward Culp's Hill, where only General Greene and his 1,310 well-dug-in Federals remained. Early was to take Johnson's advance as his signal to attack Cemetery Hill, and then Rodes would strike Cemetery Hill from the northwest.

After their long and suspenseful wait,

Johnson's three brigades rushed forward eagerly with General George (Maryland) Steuart on the left, Brigadier General John M. Jones in the center and Colonel J. M. Williams on the right. For all their determination, their progress was slowed by Federal skirmishers, rough ground and the waist-deep water of Rock Creek. By the time Johnson's troops got to the eastern foot of Culp's Hill, darkness was closing in.

When General Greene spotted Johnson's advance through the gathering dusk, he called for reinforcements, then deployed his troops. To his right yawned the trenches that had been emptied more than an hour before by the rest of XII Corps. Spreading his men thin, Greene extended his line as far as he could — about a quarter of the way into the abandoned works. Then he set his men to heaping up a traverse of logs and brush at a right angle to his line. When he was through, his men stood in a single rank

with about one foot between their elbows.

On came Johnson's Confederates, clambering up the steep, boulder-strewn hill, darting from tree to tree. As the brigades of Williams and Jones neared the Federal works, reinforcements arrived to bolster Greene's line. Wadsworth and Howard had each sent three regiments, and these helped thwart the Confederate attack; Johnson's men fell back to the base of Culp's Hill.

Three times Williams and Jones reformed and attacked, the flash of their muskets illuminating the pitch-black night, and each time they were repulsed. Over to their left, Steuart's brigade fared somewhat better, gaining the vacant Federal trenches that Greene had been unable to man. There they would huddle for the rest of the night, however, pinned down by fire from the Federals in Greene's hastily devised traverse.

Soon after Johnson began his short-lived advance, Jubal Early had put in motion the Louisiana brigade of General Harry T. Hays and the North Carolina brigade of Colonel Isaac E. Avery. As the Confederates moved over the rise that had shielded them, Federal batteries on Cemetery and Culp's Hills opened with a roar. "It was one solid crash," wrote a Federal gunner, "like a million trees falling at once."

Early's brigades made painfully slow progress against the deadly barrage, taking almost an hour to cross 700 yards of rocky ground to the saddle between Cemetery and Culp's Hills. There they routed a line of Federals behind a stone wall, but in the process Avery was shot from his horse with a musket ball through his neck. Before he died, Avery managed to dig a pencil and a scrap of paper out of his pocket and scribble: "Tell my fa-

Near the gatehouse of Evergreen Cemetery on Cemetery Hill, troops of Colonel Samuel Carroll's brigade move forward to counterattack the Louisiana Tigers, who hold Ricketts' battery in the middle distance. At left, an artillery crew gallops off the field, drawing one of Ricketts' guns to keep it from falling into Confederate hands.

ther I fell with my face to the enemy."

The attacking Confederates then came under a galling enfilading fire from the 5th Maine Battery, whose six brass smoothbores were perched on a knoll jutting from the face of Culp's Hill. Although severely shaken, the Confederates executed a textbook right oblique and began climbing Cemetery Hill. "Like an unbroken wave our maddened column rushed on," recalled Major James Beall of the 21st North Carolina. "Four of five color bearers went down. The hour was one of horror." Sweeping over another enemy line about halfway up the hill, they continued the ascent, finding that although the incline grew steeper, their progress became easier, for the Federal guns were unable to lower their elevation enough to hit them. Over the brow of the hill burst Avery's men, now commanded by Colonel Archibald Godwin of the 57th North Carolina.

Awaiting them behind a stone wall were the men of Colonel Leopold von Gilsa's hapless XI Corps brigade — who for the second time in two days took to their heels. Not far away, Generals Howard and Schurz were exchanging congratulations about the outcome of the afternoon's fighting on Cemetery Ridge. "Almost before I could tell where the assault was made," Howard recalled, "our men and the Confederates came tumbling back together."

The officers kept their heads; Schurz rounded up two regiments that were nearby and rushed them over to the spot where a wild fight was in progress for the battery commanded by Captain Michael Wiedrich. "The gunners defended themselves desperately," Schurz wrote later. "With rammers and fence rails, hand spikes and stones, they knocked down the intruders."

At one point, a Confederate officer waved his sword and cried triumphantly, "This battery is ours!" Whereupon one of Wiedrich's German-born gunners shouted, "No, dis battery is *unser*" — and clubbed down the Confederate with a spongestaff. With the arrival of Schurz and his reinforcing regiments, the North Carolinians withdrew down the slope and then disappeared into the night.

Yet the struggle for Cemetery Hill was not over. One of the regiments that had rushed to rescue Wiedrich's guns had left a gap in the line of infantry supporting the Pennsylvania battery of Captain R. Bruce Ricketts. Out of the night and through the gap poured General Hays's Louisiana Tigers, who for pure fighting ferocity had few equals in either army. Within moments, the Tigers had seized Ricketts' guns. Hays was astonished at the quiet that descended when the din of the cannonade suddenly ceased. "At that time," he wrote later, "every piece of artillery that had been firing against us was silenced."

In a few moments, the eerie quiet gave way to a babble of voices. Hays could hear a large party of men approaching, but he could not tell who they were. A volley was leveled against Hays's troops, but he ordered his men to hold their fire. The memory of Stonewall Jackson, accidentally shot to death by his own troops in the darkness at Chancellorsville, was still raw; Hays, taking no chances, refrained from firing — even after his ranks were thinned by a second volley. Then came a third, this time from so near at hand that Hays could see in the flash of musketry that the approaching men wore uniforms of Federal blue.

They were there on orders from General

A bespectacled General Meade, standing at center, conducts a war council with his general officers in the Leister house on the evening of July 2. Despite the carnage they had seen that day, reported an observer, the generals were "as calm, mild-mannered and as free from flurry or excitement as a board of commissioners met to discuss a street improvement."

Hancock. Earlier in the evening, while talking with John Gibbon on Cemetery Ridge, Hancock had heard the thunder of battle on the Federal army's right. "We ought to send some help over there," he remarked to Gibbon. And then, with sudden resolve: "Send a brigade. Send Carroll."

It was an inspired choice. The 30-year-old Colonel Samuel Sprigg Carroll belonged, according to one of his men, to that select breed of officers who attacked "wherever they got a chance, and of their own accord." Dubbed "Bricktop" by his men for the bright red hair that fringed his balding crown, he was especially admired by his troops for possessing a voice as loud as a bull elephant's — one he employed to bellow commands that were frequently and richly larded with profanity.

Crossing unfamiliar ground without a guide, Carroll had headed through the night toward the sound and flame of the guns until he encountered an artillery officer whom he knew. Asked where the Confederates were, the officer pointed in the direction of Ricketts' battery, and Carroll, trumpeting his orders, arranged his men in battle formation and attacked. Before Hays's Louisianians could recover from their commander's hesitations, Carroll's brigade was upon them. The ensuing fight lasted only a few minutes; the Confederates, outflanked, scrambled back down Cemetery Hill.

That ended the Confederate threat for the night. On Ewell's right, Rodes had not begun to maneuver his division out of Gettysburg's streets until after dark, and by the time he finally got into position, the efforts of both Johnson and Early were finished. Even so, Rodes might have attacked alone. But Brigadier General Stephen D. Ramseur, commanding Rodes's right-hand brigade, halted his men and crawled ahead to reconnoiter the western slope of Cemetery Hill. In the glow of a rising moon he saw a solid line of cannon, heavily supported by infantry, frowning down upon him.

Creeping back, Ramseur consulted with Brigadier General George Doles, on Rodes's left, and the two decided to warn Rodes of the formidable defenses they faced. As far as Rodes was concerned, the discouraging opinion of such stout fighters as Ramseur and Doles was decisive, and before long the word was passed along the Confederate ranks: "Pull back without noise."

It was then about 10:30 p.m. The uproar of the previous six and a half hours had subsided, although now and then the spiteful crack of a picket's musket could be heard above the moans and sobs of the wounded who lay sprawled by the thousands on the slopes and meadows south of Gettysburg. There was little respite for the ranking generals of the Federal army; Meade had summoned them to a council of war.

That afternoon, watching the sullen Confederate withdrawal from Cemetery Ridge, Meade had been understandably elated. "It is all right now!" he had shouted to the men around him. "It is all right now!" Later, at about 8 p.m., he had sent off a sober message to Washington: "I shall remain in my present position tomorrow."

The Federal army had survived a day of crises, but Meade was shaken by the explosive Confederate attacks. He needed to assess the situation—and sought the opinion of his commanders as to what the army should do next. The council began around 11 p.m., with at least a dozen generals crowded into the 10-by-12-foot front room of Meade's farmhouse headquarters. Illuminated by the flickering light of a single candle on a small pine table, the little parlor was soon clouded with cigar smoke.

At first the conversation was informal, with the generals trading notes on the day's battles. At length General Daniel Butterfield, Meade's chief of staff, wearied of the rambling talk. He got out a pencil and some paper and suggested that the generals give answers to three questions: Should the Army of the Potomac retreat or remain where it was? If it stayed, should it attack or continue to stand on the defensive? And, if the decision were to await an assault by Lee, how long should they wait?

In answer to the first question, the generals were of a single opinion, most forcibly expressed by Slocum: "Stay and fight it out." As for launching an immediate offensive, all were opposed. The third question—how long they should wait for Lee—drew a variety of responses, ranging from a few hours to a day.

Then Meade, who had remained generally silent, brought the session to a conclusion: The Army of the Potomac would remain in place—and fight Lee when he attacked.

Just as the meeting broke up, Meade turned to General Gibbon, whose II Corps division held the center of the Federal line. "If Lee attacks tomorrow," he said, "it will be on your front." Asked why he thought so, Meade replied with a prophetic reading of Robert E. Lee's mind: "Because he has made attacks on both our flanks and failed, and if he concludes to try it again, it will be on our center."

A Panoramic View of the Last Charge

In the Confederate attack that came to be known as Pickett's Charge, Robert E. Lee launched 12,000 infantrymen against Meade's Federals in a do-or-die effort to win the Battle of Gettysburg. The Confederates performed valiantly against overwhelming odds, but in the end they proved vincible. Less than an hour after they start-

ed, 7,500 had fallen to the enemy, the survivors were retreating in disarray and the Battle of Gettysburg was over.

Twenty years later, in 1883, French artist Paul Philippoteaux re-created Pickett's Charge in a mammoth painting. Originally 400 feet in circumference and 50 feet high, his Gettysburg Cyclorama — so called

Crossing a farm road on a black horse with his staff behind him and the blue II Corps flag flying, General Winfield Scott Hancock urges the 7th Michigan Infantry and the 1st New York Artillery forward to plug gaps in the hard-hit Angle of the Federal line on the gentle slope of Cemetery Ridge. A staff officer later wrote that the sight of the stalwart Hancock, who was badly wounded later that day, gave many soldiers the "courage longer to endure the pelting of the pitiless gale."

because its vast canvas was mounted on the interior walls of a cylindrical building — depicts the climax of the charge, when the Confederates surged momentarily across a section of the Federal line known as the Angle.

Before painting the massive work, Philippoteaux and his assistants spent several months studying the battle site and interviewing Gettysburg survivors. To ensure accuracy of terrain and scale, they made sketches and took a series of photographs from a platform that was erected just inside the Angle. The cyclorama was first exhibited in Chicago and advertised as the greatest artistic attraction ever brought to the city. In preparing later versions of the painting for display in Boston, Philadelphia and New York, Philippoteaux conferred with veterans and made additional revisions in an effort to portray with absolute faithfulness one of the horrific events of warfare. Most of the cyclorama scenes are shown on these pages.

With his rearing bay horse reined in tightly, Colonel Norman Hall raises his sword to lead the 19th Massachusetts and 42nd New York forward. Beside him, General Alexander Webb, on a white horse, looks on as the mortally wounded Lieutenant Alonzo Cushing collapses against his cannon with the vow: "I will give them one more shot, Sir." Behind Hall, just left of the clump of trees that served as a guide mark for the Confederate charge, General John Gibbon rides amidst his troops.

Surging over the Federal line at the high point of the charge, Confederates under General Lewis Armistead wave their flags *(middle distance)* triumphantly around guns they have temporarily captured. In an inaccuracy that was corrected in later versions of the painting, the mortally wounded Armistead — who was in fact on foot that day — is shown here, near his flags, falling backward off his mount. In the foreground, a Federal artillery limber from Cushing's battery heads for the rear.

In the foreground, Federal infantrymen prod Confederate prisoners rearward at bayonet point while flaunting the red and white colors they have seized. In the middle distance, Confederate General Richard Garnett — who would soon be killed — spurs on his gray horse as he brings his men forward. In the background, to the right of the Codori farm buildings on the Emmitsburg road, Confederate General George E. Pickett and his staff are seen as a small cluster of horsemen observing the battle.

Confusion breaks loose inside the Angle as a Federal caisson explodes; beyond it Confederate soldiers, loosing their high-pitched Rebel yell, swarm thickly over a stone wall to take on the 71st Pennsylvania in hand-to-hand fighting. "Every foot of ground was occupied by men engaged in mortal combat," wrote one Federal soldier; an artilleryman recalled "fighting with handspikes and rocks and anything we could get our hands on."

Confederate troops under General James Johnston Pettigrew charge across a wheat field and burst through a rail fence just north of the Angle. Against them, men of the 71st Pennsylvania stand their ground in a ragged line as Federal reinforcements rush up to bolster the endangered position. In the far distance along Seminary Ridge, smoke rises from the Confederate artillery.

The artist, Philippoteaux, painted himself into his Gettysburg epic as the Federal officer who leans against the tree with a drawn sword, surveying the scene. In the distance, Pettigrew's Confederates move across fields that one man remembered as "covered with clover as soft as a Turkish carpet."

North of the Angle, camp servants and orderlies evacuate Federal wounded on horses and mules. In the background, beyond the stone wall, skirmishers of the 111th New York pepper the advancing Confederates with flanking fire. The 12th New Jersey charges to the New Yorkers' assistance (top) past Ziegler's Grove and the Bryan farmhouse. In a letter sent home six days after the battle, a Confederate soldier wrote: "We gained nothing but

The II Corps artillery commander, Captain John G. Hazard, on horseback and accompanied by a mounted guidon-bearer, directs Captain William Arnold in deploying the five guns of Arnold's Battery A, 1st Rhode Island Light Artillery. From horse-drawn limbers, gunners run forward carrying ammunition for the cannon.

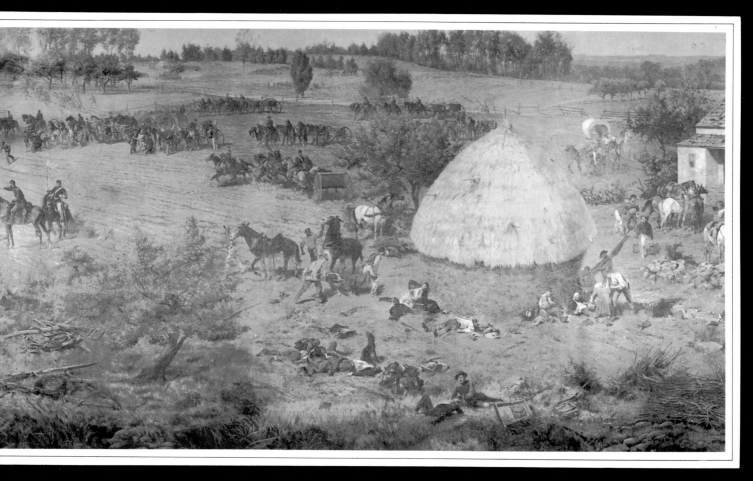

Limbers and caissons of Arnold's battery remain stationary under fire as the wounded lie about a Federal field hospital set up around a haystack. The European-style haystack is one of several minor errors made by the French artist, who was otherwise scrupulously accurate. The tall trees in the background mark the slope of Cemetery Hill, where much of the Federal reserve artillery was massed.

"In Hell or Glory"

"It is all over now. Many of us are prisoners, many are dead, many wounded, bleeding and dying. Your soldier lives and mourns and but for you, my darling, he would rather be back there with his dead, to sleep for all time in an unknown grave."

MAJOR GENERAL GEORGE PICKETT, C.S.A., TO HIS FIANCÉE, JULY 4, 1863

There was something about General George E. Pickett that smacked of the eternal sophomore. Although he had distinguished himself by his headlong bravery during the Mexican War and had been wounded at Gaines's Mill leading a charge, the glory that he so greatly coveted had eluded him. In fact, there were those who thought he had achieved his rank by cozying up to General Longstreet, his corps commander.

Longstreet did think the world of Pickett, and 35 years after the War he could still marvel at his favorite's "wondrous pulchritude and magnetic presence." Longstreet's chief of staff, Lieutenant Colonel G. Moxley Sorrel, wrote later, "I could always see how he looked after Pickett." Like almost everyone else, Sorrel thought that Pickett was "a good fellow," despite the "long ringlets that flowed over his shoulders, trimmed and highly perfumed; his beard likewise was curling and giving out the scent of Araby."

At the age of 38, Pickett was ecstatically in love with a teen-age Virginia beauty named LaSalle Corbell, to whom he would be wed soon after Gettysburg. During his absences from her, Pickett all but drowned the young lady in a flood of sentimental blather. She was, he wrote her, "the sweetest, loveliest flower that ever blossomed." And on the march into Pennsylvania, he avowed that "every tramp-tramp-tramp is a thought-thought-thought of my darling."

Pickett's division, with fewer than 6,000 men in its 15 Virginia regiments, was one of the smallest in the Army of Northern Virginia. It also had little experience as a fighting unit: Formed the previous September, the division had been held in reserve at Fredericksburg; it had been in southern Virginia during the Chancellorsville Campaign; and when the fighting started at Gettysburg, it had been guarding the army's supply wagons at Chambersburg.

Relieved from that assignment on July 2, the division toiled across South Mountain and at about 6 p.m. halted four miles west of Gettysburg. Pickett sent word to Lee that the men were weary, but if necessary they could resume their march and pitch into the fight. "Tell General Pickett," Lee responded, "I shall not want him this evening; to let his men rest, and I will send him word when I want him."

Lee's plans evolved that night: Longstreet, reinforced by Pickett's three brigades, would attack the Federal center the next morning, while Ewell assailed the enemy's right. Both would launch their assaults from ground they had wrested from the Federals, Longstreet driving from the Peach Orchard and the Devil's Den toward Cemetery Ridge, and Ewell striking southward from the trenches that Johnson had seized that evening on Culp's Hill.

But at dawn, just as Pickett's division approached the battlefield, Lee heard his plans disintegrate; a deep growl of gunfire from the direction of Culp's Hill informed him that Ewell was already engaged.

At Gettysburg on the afternoon of July 3, this 12-pounder Napoleon belonging to Battery B, 1st Rhode Island Artillery, was damaged by an exploding shell that killed two of the gunners. When the survivors tried to load the piece, the round became stuck in the dented muzzle and could not be extracted.

The Federals had started the fight. Although Meade was determined to keep a defensive posture, he allowed one exception: During the night the XII Corps had been sent back to Culp's Hill with orders to drive Johnson's Confederates from the captured trenches. To that end 20 guns had been placed on high ground west of the Baltimore Pike so that they enfiladed Johnson's lines. At about 4:30 a.m., as dawn broke through misty clouds, the artillery opened fire to prepare the way for an infantry charge.

Johnson, too, had been reinforced during the night — by General James A. Walker's redoubtable Stonewall Brigade and three other brigades. Under the savage bombardment, he could not stay where he was. But he would not withdraw, and so at 8 a.m. he attacked. For more than three hours a vicious struggle raged at close quarters, amid what one Federal officer called "great rocks that lie there like a herd of sleeping elephants." From the cover of log breastworks many Union soldiers fired more than 160 rounds into the advancing Confederates. The result was disastrous for the attackers. "The wonder is," wrote General Alpheus Williams of XII Corps later, "that the rebels persisted so long in an attempt that in the first half hour must have seemed useless."

Yet persist they did. General John M. Jones was wounded at the head of his brigade, and his men fell back. Colonel Edward A. O'Neal's brigade struggled up the hill but was pinned down before it could reach the Federal positions. Then the Stonewall Brigade tried and failed. Still unwilling to call it quits, Johnson at 10 a.m. ordered the brigades of Junius Daniel and Maryland Steuart to attack. Both were stopped before they reached the breastworks.

Time and again, the Confederates rallied and charged, their officers in the lead. Major Henry Kyd Douglas, Stonewall Jackson's longtime aide, was shot through the shoulder, pulled from his horse and captured. General Johnson's chief of staff, Major Benjamin W. Leigh, spurred to within feet of the Federal breastworks, where horse and rider fell riddled with bullets. When the troops on Steuart's left wavered, he ran to the front of the 1st Maryland Battalion and led them forward. "The little battalion never wavered nor hesitated," one officer recalled, "but kept on, closing up its ranks as great gaps were torn through them, and many of the brave fellows never stopped until they had passed through the enemy's first line or had fallen dead or wounded as they reached it." The Marylanders lost more than half of their 400 men; one soldier killed himself with a shot in the head rather than surrender.

Finally, at about 11 a.m., a Federal countercharge swept down on Johnson's left, and the Confederates were forced to withdraw east across Rock Creek. Johnson's division — and for that matter, Ewell's corps — would do no more fighting at Gettysburg. For decades thereafter on Culp's Hill a ghostly forest would stand, its trees shorn of their limbs and stripped of their bark by flying metal — testimony to the savagery of a contest that would nevertheless be overshadowed by events still to come.

On hearing the Federal bombardment, Lee had ridden to Seminary Ridge to find Longstreet, whose words of greeting must have tested Lee's composure: "General, I have had my scouts out all night, and I find that you still have an excellent opportunity to move around to the right of Meade's army, and maneuver him into attacking us." That was, of course, the plan that Longstreet had been urging all along and that Lee had rejected several times. Grimly, the commanding general pointed to the Federal lines. "The enemy is there," he said, "and I am going to strike him."

Still Longstreet objected, especially to the use of Hood's and McLaws' divisions in the assault. As he wrote later, "To have rushed forward my two divisions, then carrying bloody noses from their terrible conflict the day before, would have been madness." On this point Lee gave in, and agreed to modify his plan.

The assault would be made by Pickett's fresh division, along with two others: Henry Heth's, and a combination of four brigades from Dorsey Pender's and Richard Anderson's divisions. At Lee's direction, the attackers would guide on a little, umbrella-shaped clump of oak trees on the otherwise bare crest of Cemetery Ridge, near the center of the Federal line.

The whole plan had a makeshift air about it. Heth's division had suffered casualties of at least 40 per cent and was severely shaken. Among the wounded were Heth and all brigade commanders except Pettigrew, who now led the division. The third attack division was placed under the command of 61-year-old Major General Isaac Trimble. Not only was Trimble a complete stranger to the brigades he would lead, but he joined them after they were deployed — too late to correct what turned out to be fatal flaws.

With the plan set, Longstreet asked how many men would participate in the attack. When Lee said about 15,000 — an estimate that turned out to be more than 20 per cent high — Longstreet made a final, impassioned plea: "General, I have been a soldier all my life. I have been with soldiers engaged in fights by couples, by squads, companies, regiments, divisions, and armies, and should know, as well as anyone, what soldiers can do. It is my opinion that no 15,000 men ever arrayed for battle can take that position."

Lee refused to budge. By Longstreet's account, the commanding general "seemed a little impatient, so I said nothing more. Never was I so depressed as upon that day."

By 9 a.m. the attacking forces were forming their lines of battle in the cover of the woods northwest of the Peach Orchard, with Pickett's division on the right, Pettigrew's on the left and Trimble's trailing in support on Pettigrew's right rear. There was a space of nearly a quarter mile between Pickett's left and the right of Pettigrew, a gap that could not be effectively closed in the woods. Thus Pickett's line would have to bear to the left while advancing across the field — a very tricky proposition indeed.

While supervising these arrangements,

Early on the battle's third day, General George "Maryland" Steuart leads his 1st Maryland Battalion in a futile and bloody assault on the Federal breastworks atop Culp's Hill. After the setback, one soldier wrote, "General Steuart was heartbroken. Tears stealing down his cheeks, he was heard repeatedly to exclaim: 'My poor boys! My poor boys!'"

Lee apparently became aware for the first time just how badly some of his brigades had been battered. Peering at the ranks of exhausted men, he said to Trimble: "Many of these poor boys should go to the rear; they are not fit for duty." Yet there could be no turning back, and as Lee rode away he said, almost to himself: "The attack must succeed."

Meanwhile, Longstreet's artillerists prepared to blast a path for the infantrymen. The responsibility for the bombardment fell upon 27-year-old Colonel E. Porter Alexander. Although only a battalion commander, Alexander had performed brilliantly at Fredericksburg and Chancellorsville; Longstreet clearly had more faith in him than in the corps's senior artillery

commander, Colonel J. B. Walton.

Alexander placed 75 guns along a front extending 1,300 yards northward from the Peach Orchard; eight others were located to the south to cover the flank of the attacking infantry. Several hundred yards to the left and rear of Alexander's main line were 60 of A. P. Hill's cannon and, beyond them, 24 of Ewell's. All told, the Confederates deployed about 170 guns, each with 130 to 150 rounds of ammunition available; everything was ready for the most colossal cannonade in the nation's history.

Just then, Alexander received a strange and disturbing note from Longstreet. In it, the corps commander seemed to place on Alexander the burden of assessing the results of the bombardment and deciding whether

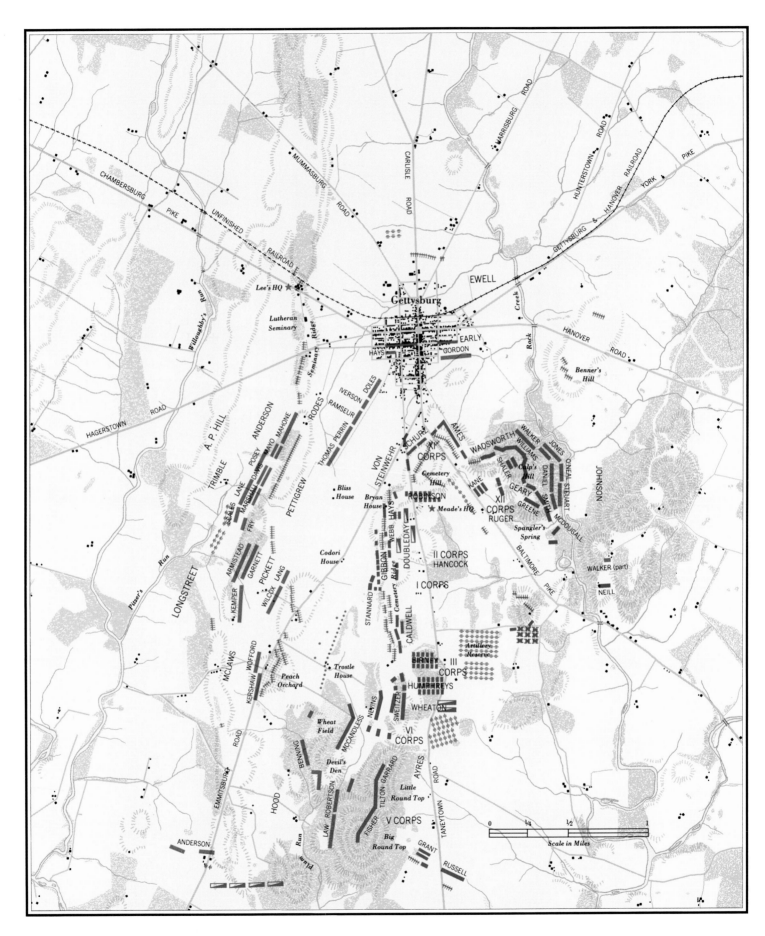

Colonel E. Porter Alexander, the brilliant Confederate artillerist who directed the bombardment of the Federal position on Cemetery Ridge, doubted the wisdom of Lee's climactic frontal assault. He later wrote, "It seemed madness to undertake an advance over open ground against the center of that line."

Shortly before dawn on July 3, Richard Ewell's corps assailed the Federal right flank at Culp's Hill. In six hours of fighting, every Confederate assault on the well-fortified position was repulsed by the Federal XII Corps. At 1 p.m., the Confederate artillery opposite the Federal center on Cemetery Ridge began a heavy bombardment, and two hours later one of Longstreet's divisions and two of A. P. Hill's attacked the Federal II Corps on the ridge.

the infantry charge should be made. Appalled by his dilemma — to cancel Lee's assault was unthinkable, yet so was open defiance of Longstreet — Alexander protested that the decision should be made before the guns opened fire. Once again, Longstreet instructed the colonel to determine whether "the artillery has the desired effect of driving the enemy's off."

It was a determination that the young officer felt he could not make; he could only follow the plan of battle. "When our fire is at its best," he wrote Longstreet, "I will advise General Pickett to advance." Reluctantly, Longstreet sent the order to begin the bombardment. At precisely 1 p.m., Alexander remembered, the roar of artillery "burst in on the silence, almost as suddenly as the full notes of an organ would fill a church."

In the 90° heat and smothering humidity, the Federals on Cemetery Ridge had passed much of the morning moving as if in slow motion; some had trouble staying awake. "We dozed in the heat," recalled an officer, "and lolled upon the ground, with half open eyes. Our horses were hitched to the trees munching some oats. Time was heavy."

At about 9 a.m., General Meade rode over to discuss the situation with Hancock. For

no apparent reason, Meade had decided that the Confederates probably would not attack the center of his line, as he had predicted the previous evening, but would instead hit his left in the vicinity of the Round Tops.

The army was accordingly disposed. Massed on and near the Round Tops were V Corps, the remnants of III Corps and most of VI Corps, now recovered from its arduous march. With XI and XII Corps and much of I Corps still occupying Cemetery and Culp's Hills, that left the defense of the center, on Cemetery Ridge, to two divisions of Hancock's II Corps, along with part of Doubleday's I Corps division. No more than 5,750 infantrymen were stretched along the half-mile front that would bear the brunt of a charge by 12,000 very determined Confederates.

At the northern part of the ridge, in front of Ziegler's Grove and an adjacent orchard, General Alexander Hays's II Corps division was in position behind a dilapidated stone fence that ran southward along the foot of the slope. At a point about 250 feet north of the little clump of oaks that was the target for the Confederate attack, the fence turned to the west for 239 feet. Then it jogged back toward the south, forming a salient that would achieve sinister fame as the Angle.

Within the salient and north of the clump of trees was Battery A, 4th U.S. Artillery — six 3-inch ordnance rifles under Lieutenant Alonzo H. Cushing. His artillerymen were supported by the 71st Pennsylvania of Alexander Webb's Philadelphia Brigade. Along the wall in front of the trees was another of Webb's regiments, the largely Irish 69th Pennsylvania, which supported a Rhode Island battery of Napoleons commanded by Lieutenant T. Fred Brown. Another of

A Collision of Cavalry

As Pickett's Charge unfolded along Cemetery Ridge, cavalry forces clashed three miles east of Gettysburg in a bitter contest that could have changed the course of the battle.

Around noon, General Jeb Stuart deployed his four brigades — 6,300 men — in the woods on Cress's Ridge, bent on pushing westward across an open plain and into the rear of the Federal army. Across this plain, along Hanover Road, were arrayed 4,500 Federal troopers — two brigades of David Gregg's division and George Custer's brigade of Judson Kilpatrick's division.

After dismounted horsemen fought in the plain, Stuart sent the 1st Virginia on a headlong charge down the ridge. Gregg answered with a countercharge by the 7th Michigan that stopped the Confederates. Not to be denied, Stuart committed most of Wade Hampton's and Fitzhugh Lee's brigades in a narrow column of squadrons. The polish of the advancing Confederate horsemen drew a murmur of admiration from the Federals. "They marched with well-aligned fronts and steady reins," an appreciative Federal wrote later. "Their polished saber-blades dazzled in the sun." But for all its precision, Stuart's long column proved dangerously vulnerable. Shell and shrapnel tore holes along its length.

Then Gregg ordered the 1st Michigan to charge the head of Stuart's column. Custer took the lead, brandishing his saber and shouting, "Come on, you Wolverines!" The 1st Michigan rushed forward with a fierce yell, and the enemy horsemen raced into each other with a crash one participant likened to "falling timber. So violent was the collision that many horses were turned end over end and crushed their riders beneath them."

As fierce hand-to-hand fighting ensued, Union forces closed in from the flanks and ripped through Stuart's column from both sides. Captain William E. Miller's squadron of the 3rd Pennsylvania Cavalry, attacking from the east, severed the rear of the column from the main body and drove it back.

The Confederates soon gave way under the furious frontal and flank attacks and punishing artillery. They retreated to Cress's Ridge, and the battle subsided. In three hours of fighting, at least 181 Confederates (one brigade failed to report losses) and 254 Federals were killed, wounded or captured. Neither side lost ground, and both would claim victory. But Gregg's brilliant parry prevented Stuart from breaking through and diverting Federal forces from the main battle along Cemetery Ridge. A proud Federal cavalryman would subsequently boast: "We saved the day at the most critical moment of the battle of Gettysburg."

A Union cavalryman sabers a Confederate guidon-bearer (*center*) amid turbulent close-quarter fighting. General Custer wrote of the Union counterattack: "I challenge the annals of war to produce a more brilliant charge."

Webb's regiments, the 72nd Pennsylvania, was in reserve behind the stand of oaks. The other II Corps division, under John Gibbon, extended the line to the south. With no wall in front of them, his men had thrown up a slight barrier of earth about knee high.

Meanwhile, General Henry Hunt, the Federal artillery chief, had placed 77 guns along the crest of Cemetery Ridge, with well over half of the pieces on the southern end. Five batteries — 25 guns — defended the crucial center. Another 50 cannon were posted on Cemetery Hill and Little Round Top, within range of the Federal center.

Around 11 a.m., as the fighting on Culp's Hill subsided, an oppressive silence had fallen over the field. "It became as still as the Sabbath day," wrote one Union soldier. Recalled another, "It was a queer sight to see men look at each other without speaking; the change was so great men seemed to go on tiptoe not knowing how to act." Still another would remember that he could "distinctly hear the hum of the honeybees working."

For a favored few, there was even a good meal. A couple of Gibbon's foragers had scrounged what the general described as "an old and tough rooster," with which they made a stew. Gibbon invited Meade, Hancock, Newton, Pleasonton and some aides to share the repast. They sat in the shade of a tree near Meade's headquarters behind Cemetery Ridge, savoring of their stew and, later, puffing on cigars. After a while, Meade and some of the others departed. But several were still taking their ease when the Confederate batteries opened. Suddenly, Gibbon recalled, "the air was all murderous iron."

Among the first casualties was an orderly who had been serving butter to the commanders: He was cut in half by a flying shell.

The puffs of smoke and flashes of fire that traveled rapidly down the line of Confederate artillery reminded one Federal soldier on Cemetery Hill of "the 'powder snakes' we boys used to touch off on the 4th of July." Another would remember the sight of small birds fluttering about in confusion as the world around them was ripped apart. General Hunt, the coolly professional artilleryman, was enthralled by a spectacle that seemed to him "indescribably grand."

With a fine sense of theater, Hancock set out to show every soldier in II Corps that "his general was behind him in the storm." Sitting ramrod-straight on his prancing horse, he rode down the line. More than 20 years later General Abner Doubleday would write: "I can almost fancy I can see Hancock again, followed by a single orderly displaying his corps flag, while the missiles from a hundred pieces of artillery tore up the ground around him." Finally, a brigadier admonished him: "General, the corps commander ought not to risk his life that way." Replied Hancock: "There are times when a corps commander's life does not count."

When Hancock saw that the Confederates were concentrating their fire around the little clump of trees, he sent word to Hunt to dispatch two more batteries there. Hunt complied, but in fact, he and Hancock were at odds throughout much of the cannonade. Hunt, painfully aware of the need to conserve ammunition to meet the infantry charge he knew was coming, ordered his guns along Cemetery Ridge to hold their fire. Only the batteries on Cemetery Hill and Little Round Top replied to the enemy's guns.

Hancock, on the other hand, knew all too well how the morale of infantrymen suffers in a bombardment when their own guns stay

During the bombardment preceding Lee's offensive on the afternoon of July 3, Confederate infantrymen huddle behind a low breastwork of fence rails and logs on the west slope of Seminary Ridge. The foot soldiers bore the brunt of the counterfire by Federal artillery; before the attack, one of James Kemper's regiments had already lost 88 men.

silent. After about 15 minutes, he overrode Hunt and ordered the II Corps's artillery commander, Captain John Hazard, to start firing. The five II Corps batteries complied with great gusto, but on the southern end of the ridge, 36 guns from the artillery reserve remained mute. They were commanded by Lieutenant Colonel Freeman McGilvery, who had the day before shown considerable courage against the enemy; now he demonstrated that he was not afraid of the formidable Hancock either. Contending that he could take orders only from Hunt, McGilvery ignored Hancock's command.

Despite its awesome volume, the Confederate cannonade was, in the words of a Federal officer, "by no means as effective as it should have been, nine-tenths of their shot passing over our men." With their targets obscured by clouds of gun smoke billowing over the field, many of the Confederate guns were shooting high — although not by much. "It seemed that nothing four feet from the ground could live," wrote one Union soldier. And another recalled, "All we had to do was flatten out a little thinner, and our empty stomachs did not prevent that."

But many of the shells that passed over the men on Cemetery Ridge found other targets, among them Meade's headquarters. Before long, 16 horses lay dead or maimed in the yard outside the headquarters house; one shell smashed through the roof, and another tore through the door, narrowly missing the army's commander. General Butterfield was wounded by a shell fragment. Meade and his staff were forced to move southeastward to a safer location. The reserve artillery and the army's ammunition train, massed on the far side of the ridge, were similarly threatened. Reluctantly, Brigadier General Robert O. Tyler, commander of the reserve artillery, ordered them moved a half mile farther south — thereby increasing the time required for reserve batteries and fresh supplies of ammunition to reach the front.

The Union batteries that had been ordered to fire away on Cemetery Ridge made easy marks, even in the smoke; during the 90-minute cannonade, they were badly mauled. Captain James McKay Rorty's New York battery, on the southern end of Gibbon's line, was especially hard hit. "The scene was more than dramatic," an officer observed. "With guns dismounted, caissons blown up, and rapidly losing men and horses, the intrepid commander moved from gun to gun as coolly as if at a West Point review." Finally

As he awaited the order to advance, the flamboyant Major General George Pickett was uncharacteristically subdued. "My brave Virginians are to attack in front," he scrawled in a hasty note to his fiancée. "Oh, may God in mercy help me as He never helped before!"

Rorty himself was killed. Within the Angle, three of Cushing's ammunition chests were hit and exploded, wrecking the limbers. A gun in Brown's Rhode Island battery was struck on the muzzle while being loaded; the blast tore off a soldier's head and ripped away the left arm of Private Alfred Gardner, a devout man who died crying: "Glory to God! I am happy! Hallelujah!"

Shortly after 2:30 p.m., the Federals made a decision that would change the course of the battle. Artillery chief Hunt was approached on Cemetery Ridge by the commander of the XI Corps batteries, Major Thomas W. Osborn. It had occurred to Osborn that General Meade might actually be eager for Lee's infantry brigades to attack. Hunt confirmed that he had heard Meade express just such an attitude.

"If this is so," said Osborn, "I would cease fire at once, and the enemy could reach but one conclusion, that of our being driven from the hill." The idea of luring the Confederates into an early assault was appealing to Hunt, who had been urging from the outset that ammunition be conserved. Soon the order to cease fire was passed down the line, and one by one, the Federal batteries fell silent.

At the same time it became apparent that Brown's shattered battery — with all its officers killed or wounded, its ammunition nearly exhausted and scarcely enough men left to work its three remaining guns — could not survive the ordeal. Ordered to withdraw, the battery did so, to be replaced by a fresh battery under Captain Andrew Cowan.

On Seminary Ridge, Colonel Alexander spotted Brown's withdrawal, saw some of Cushing's damaged guns in the Angle being pushed to the rear and noted that the spew of flame and smoke from the Federal guns was diminishing.

Until then, Alexander had been convinced that the Confederates were getting the worst of the artillery duel. Federal shells were decimating the infantry waiting in the woods behind the Confederate artillery line. "There were to be seen at almost every moment of time," wrote one Confederate, "guns, swords, haversacks, human flesh flying above the earth, which now trembled beneath us as shaken by an earthquake." As many as 500 men were killed or wounded in Pickett's division alone.

But once Colonel Alexander saw to his vast delight that the fire from the ridge was fading and that some of the guns were withdrawing, he reached a fateful conclusion: The time was ripe for an assault. Hastily, Alexander scribbled a message to Pickett: "The 18 guns have been driven off. For God's sake, come quick, or we cannot support you. Ammunition nearly out."

On receiving the note at about 3 p.m., Pickett rode to see Longstreet. "General," Pickett asked, "shall I advance?" Overwhelmed by an emotion that rendered him unable — or unwilling — to reply, Longstreet merely bowed his head. Taking this to be affirmation, Pickett declared: "I shall lead my division forward, sir."

As Pickett departed, Cadmus Wilcox rode up to him, offering the contents of a flask. "Pickett, take a drink with me," he said. "In an hour you'll be in hell or glory." Pickett declined, saying he had pledged abstinence to his LaSalle. Taking his place in front of the division, Pickett addressed the men in a loud, clear voice: "Charge the enemy and remember old Virginia!" And then:

"Forward! Guide center! March!"

Under orders neither to fire nor to emit their fearsome Rebel yell, the three divisions of Confederates advanced through the woods in eerie silence at a steady pace of about 100 yards per minute, blue flags flapping over Pickett's regiments and red colors over Pettigrew's and Trimble's. Longstreet, seated on a rail fence, watched them go.

Brigadier General James Kemper, a 40-year-old former Virginia legislator who had been fighting since First Bull Run, led Pickett's right-front brigade. To Kemper's left, on a black horse, rode Brigadier General Richard B. Garnett. Though severely in-

jured by a kick from his horse and barely able to walk, the 45-year-old Garnett was more than willing to risk his life to refute the unjust charges of cowardice that Stonewall Jackson had brought against him after the Battle of Kernstown. Behind Garnett's brigade was that of 46-year-old, gray-bearded Brigadier General Lewis A. Armistead. Waving his black slouch hat from the tip of his sword, Armistead advanced on foot against the line commanded by one of his dearest friends from the Regular Army, General Hancock. Pickett rode about 20 yards to the rear, the proper place for a division commander; the fond Longstreet would remember him advancing "gracefully, with his jaunty cap raked well over his right ear."

To a Federal officer near the clump of trees, the oncoming tide of men in gray had "the appearance of being fearfully irresistible." Instructing his troops to hold their fire until the last possible moment, Colonel Dennis O'Kane of the 69th Pennsylvania added emotionally, "Let your work this day be for victory or death!" Farther north on the line, General Hays formed his men behind the stone wall and put them through a brisk drill to keep them from growing skittish while waiting for the blow to fall.

Once clear of the woods, Pickett's division at an order faced 45 degrees left and headed northeast to close with Pettigrew's division. In so doing, Pickett exposed his right flank to raking fire from six Parrotts on Little Round Top and McGilvery's guns on the southern end of Cemetery Ridge. "We could not help hitting them at every shot," said one of McGilvery's officers. According to Major Charles Peyton, with the 19th Virginia in Garnett's brigade, the Federal cannon fired "with fearful effect, sometimes as many as ten men being killed and wounded by the bursting of a single shell."

Nearing the Emmitsburg road, the division came to a shallow swale that provided partial cover. But men were still falling as the regiments halted and, with a parade-ground aplomb that awed the Federal troops on the ridge, closed the gaps that had been blasted in their ranks and re-dressed their lines.

On the Confederate left, Colonel Robert Mayo's brigade of Pettigrew's division had for unknown reasons been slow to emerge from the woods and was just catching up when it came under fire from the XI Corps batteries on Cemetery Hill. Almost immedi-

In a view from Seminary Ridge, Confederate battle lines sweep forward to attack smoke-shrouded Cemetery Ridge, crowned by Ziegler's Grove at left and the copse of trees at right. Federal artillery on Cemetery Hill (*center background*) adds its fire to that of the II Corps batteries on the ridge.

ately, men began to trickle toward the rear — and then disaster struck the brigade.

On the afternoon before, the 8th Ohio, part of Colonel Samuel S. Carroll's brigade, had been sent west of the Emmitsburg road to form a skirmish line. Unlike most skirmishers, who are expected to withdraw before a strong advance, the 8th Ohio, under Lieutenant Colonel Franklin Sawyer, had been instructed by the bellicose Carroll to hold its ground. That evening Carroll had gone to help defend Culp's Hill, leaving his order in effect — and so it remained.

If the 8th Ohio's men had stayed where they were, the Confederate line of advance would have swept past them to the south. But Sawyer, a man who took orders seriously, clearly believed that he had been sent forward to get into a fight, not to stay out of one. And so, while onlookers on Cemetery Ridge speculated that he must be drunk, Sawyer faced his men south, waited until the enemy was passing about 100 yards from his little line and then opened fire on a Confederate brigade that outnumbered his understrength regiment by about 5 to 1.

Sawyer's quixotic effort had an immediate, astonishing effect: Mayo's brigade, already severely shaken by Federal artillery fire, broke and ran for the safety of Seminary Ridge. The Ohioans charged forward, capturing 200 prisoners. The rout exposed the left of Joseph Davis' Mississippi brigade. Those troops, now caught in a heavy cross fire from left and front, began to crumble.

The units on Pettigrew's right continued to advance in good order, however, and just before reaching the Emmitsburg road, Pickett's left linked up with them. Maintaining its deliberate pace, still withholding its fire, the united Confederate force approached the

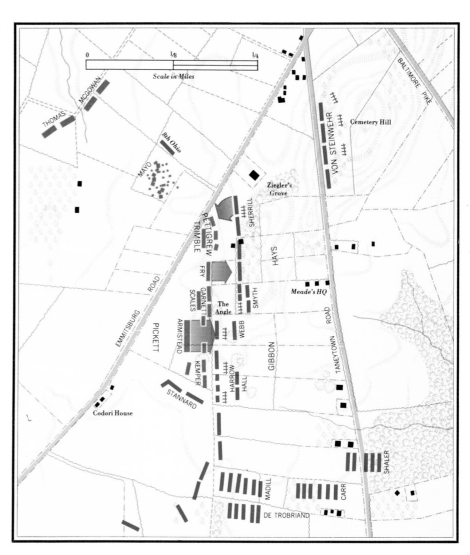

long, gentle slope that led to the crest of Cemetery Ridge. As the gray lines started up the rise, a sword-waving lieutenant expressed the heart's desire of them all: "Home, boys, home!" he cried. "Remember, home is over beyond those hills!"

But thousands of them would never get home. Especially on the left, the advancing brigades were taking terrible punishment from the Federal guns on Cemetery Hill and Lieutenant George Woodruff's battery at Ziegler's Grove. And now the Confederates

At 3:30 p.m., the Confederate divisions of George Pickett, James Johnston Pettigrew and Isaac Trimble struck the line of Winfield Scott Hancock's II Corps on Cemetery Ridge. Although the attackers were enfiladed on both flanks, a group of 150 men led by Lewis Armistead temporarily broke the line of Alexander Webb's Federal brigade at the Angle. After 20 more minutes of fighting, counterattacking troops of Norman Hall's brigade plugged the gap, and the battered Confederates retreated.

Although Pickett came unscathed through the charge that bears his name, all three of his brigade commanders were casualties. James Kemper was shot from his horse and crippled for life. Lewis Armistead was fatally wounded at the Angle. Richard Garnett's body was never found; years later his sword was recovered in a Baltimore pawnshop.

GENERAL RICHARD B. GARNETT

GENERAL LEWIS A. ARMISTEAD

GENERAL JAMES L. KEMPER

were approaching the stone wall, behind which General Hays and his men waited.

Hays, who actually enjoyed mortal combat, was having the time of his life. As the Confederate forces neared, he enjoined his troops: "Now, boys, look out; you will see some fun." Hays waited until the enemy brigade under Colonel Birkett D. Fry got tangled up with a pair of stout rail fences about 200 yards to his front. Then Hays bellowed "Fire!" and from his line there blazed the concentrated fury of 1,700 muskets and 11 cannon.

A Federal officer wrote later that the Confederate lines "underwent an instantaneous transformation. They were at once enveloped in a dense cloud of dust. Arms, heads, blankets, guns and knapsacks were tossed into the clear air. A moan went up from the field distinctly to be heard amid the storm of battle."

Colonel James K. Marshall, leading Pettigrew's only intact brigade, was shot dead from his horse. Pettigrew himself took an ugly wound in his right hand. The doughty old Colonel Fry crossed the stone wall just north of the Angle, flag in hand. There he went down with a thigh wound, still shouting encouragement: "Go on! It will not last five minutes longer!"

The excitable Hays had a keen tactical eye, and he presently spotted a splendid opportunity. The flight of Mayo's brigade and the drastic shrinking of Davis' had contracted the left of the oncoming Confederate line until it was overlapped by Hays's troops. Immediately Hays ordered his northernmost regiment, the 126th New York, along with a section of Woodruff's battery, to wheel left so that they faced south. Woodruff fell with a mortal wound as this maneuver was being executed, but within minutes his two brass Napoleons and 400 of the New Yorkers' muskets were pouring a lethal flanking fire into Pettigrew's remaining troops.

On spotting Hays's move, Hancock was struck by the possibility of a double envelopment — the dream of every infantry commander. To see if a maneuver similar to Hays's could be executed at the other end of the Federal line, Hancock galloped southward — where, as it turned out, just such an envelopment was already being tried.

The men of Brigadier General George J. Stannard's Vermont brigade had been feeling edgy about their assigned position on the far left of Meade's Cemetery Ridge line. The ground was low there, but about 100 yards to their front was a little knoll that looked much more secure. Despite Hancock's expressed fears that they would be dangerously exposing themselves, two of Stannard's regiments, the 13th and 14th Vermont, had gone out in front of the rest of the army and had begun piling up dirt and brush to fortify the hillock. Later, they were joined there by the 16th Vermont, which had fallen back from the Federal skirmish line.

Initially, Pickett's Confederates had been heading straight toward Stannard's brigade. A Vermont private recalled spotting them "as they reached the crest of Seminary Ridge a full half-mile away, at first a horse and rider, then glistening bayonets and flags and banners waving and fluttering in the sultry air." But after changing direction to join Pettigrew's line, Pickett's troops moved at an angle across Stannard's front, and the Vermonters were able to pour damaging fire into their ranks. It became apparent that the Confederates meant to bypass Stannard's men and strike Cemetery Ridge farther north.

Whether it was Hancock or Stannard who was responsible for what happened next was never determined; both would claim credit. In any case, just as Pickett's brigades were starting up Cemetery Ridge the Vermonters wheeled toward the north, halted within easy range and fired a volley into the 24th Virginia on James Kemper's right flank. From his position higher on the slope, Doubleday saw Stannard's attack, waved his hat wildly and shouted, "Glory to God, glory to God! See the Vermonters go it!"

Shying away from the unexpected fire on its right, Kemper's brigade began crowding to its left, into the brigades of Garnett and Armistead. Desperate to get his men back on track, Kemper sought to urge them toward the main enemy line to the east. "There are the guns, boys," he cried. "Go for them!" But in the wild confusion, he inadvertently pointed his sword to the north, thereby accelerating the stampede in that direction. Hardly had he made the fateful gesture than he fell from his horse with a bullet near his spine that left him partially paralyzed.

Shrinking from the lethal flanking fire on both right and left, the attacking Confederates continued to herd toward the center. Soon the better part of five brigades became, in the word of one Confederate officer, "a mingled mass, from fifteen to thirty deep." Richard Garnett was striving to restore order, riding up and down exhorting the troops, when he disappeared in the inferno. Private James Clay of the 18th Virginia later wrote, "The last I saw of General Garnett he was astride his big black charger in the forefront of the charge and near the stone wall, gallantly waving his hat and cheering the men on." Moments later Garnett's frenzied, riderless horse came dashing back, horribly

Brigadier General Alexander Webb's brigade bore the brunt of the Confederate assault on the Angle. When one of his regiments broke and another refused to advance, Webb ran toward the Confederates alone. "I almost wished to get killed," he later wrote. Wounded in the thigh, he was awarded the Medal of Honor for his bravery.

wounded and covered with blood. The general was never seen again.

The jostling mob of Pickett's division was now directly in front of the Angle and the clump of trees. In the Angle, 250 soldiers of the 71st Pennsylvania blazed away from behind the stone wall. In front of the clump of trees, the 69th Pennsylvania, supported by the five guns of Cowan's 1st New York battery, fired volley after volley into the Confederate ranks.

The guns of Cushing and Cowan were cutting wagon-wide swaths in the roiling mass of Confederates. Federal artillery chief Hunt was with Cowan's battery, hysterically shouting "See 'em! See 'em!" as he fired his revolver into the Virginians swarming over the wall. Then Hunt's horse fell, pinning him to the ground, and the Confederates, led by Colonel James Hodges of the 14th Virgin-

In this view of Pickett's Charge by artist Thomas Nast, men of Webb's embattled brigade strive to hold their ground, while troops of the 19th Massachusetts and 42nd New York charge to their relief at right.

ia, surged to within 10 paces of Cowan's guns. At that moment Cowan yelled "Fire!" With a thunderous roar the five guns spewed out double-shotted canister, and when the smoke cleared not a Confederate in front of the battery remained standing. In places, their mutilated bodies lay three deep.

During the Confederate bombardment, Cushing had suffered a shoulder wound but remained in action. Then a shell fragment tore into his groin. He ordered his one serviceable gun wheeled down to the wall and was shouting orders to his gunners when a bullet entered through his open mouth. As he crumpled dead to the ground, his gun fired its last load of canister. The Confederates swarmed over the wall, and Cushing's gunners hastily abandoned their position.

The disorganized Confederates were thus offered a priceless opportunity, but to seize it

they needed a leader — and now, pushing through the mob came General Armistead, his hat still on the tip of his sword. "Come on, boys," he cried, "Give them the cold steel! Who will follow me?"

Armistead leaped over the wall, followed by a mob of officers and men, and the spine-tingling Rebel yell shrilled across the field. In the face of this onslaught, the 71st Pennsylvania broke. In his instant of greatest glory, Armistead reached possessively for the barrel of one of Cushing's guns — and fell, mortally wounded by a rifle ball. His men pressed on, some of them overrunning part of the 69th Pennsylvania and reaching the copse of trees before their screams of triumph were cut short by a Federal volley.

It came from the 72nd Pennsylvania, brought forward by General Webb just as the 71st collapsed. The first volley from the

72nd stopped the Confederate rush, though many stayed within the Angle while others took cover on the west side of the stone wall and continued to fire. Webb then ordered the 72nd to charge. No one moved. Waving his sword, Webb repeated the command. Again, the men refused to budge. Wild with frustration, Webb tried to seize the regimental flag; its bearer would not yield it. The two wrestled ignominiously for it until Webb, in utter disgust, went down to the clump of trees to spur on the 69th Pennsylvania.

Other Federals were now pushing into the fight. On his way to Stannard's line, General Hancock was stopped by Colonel Arthur Devereux of the 19th Massachusetts. That regiment, along with the 42nd New York, had been posted southeast of the clump of trees. "See, general," said Devereux, "they have broken through; the colors are coming over the stone wall; let me go in there!" Snapped Hancock: "Go in there pretty God-damned quick!"

Following Colonel Devereux, the 19th Massachusetts and the 42nd New York crashed into the Confederates within the Angle. A Massachusetts soldier remembered the collision: "The two lines come together with a shock which stops them both and causes a slight rebound. Foot to foot, body to body and man to man they struggled, pushed and strived and killed. The mass of

The panoramic *Repulse of Long-street's Assault*, by artist James Walker, was based on wartime sketches and interviews with survivors. Walker painstakingly represented 170 identifiable figures on the canvas. One of them is the mortally wounded General Armistead, behind Federal lines in the foreground, who is handing his pocket watch to an officer to pass along to General Hancock, his old friend, for safekeeping.

wounded and heaps of dead entangled the feet of the contestants, and, underneath the trampling mass, wounded men who could no longer stand, struggled, fought, shouted and killed — hatless, coatless, drowned in sweat, black with powder, red with blood, with fiendish yells and strange oaths they blindly plied the work of slaughter."

Within minutes every Confederate who had crossed the wall was killed or captured. Then at last, one by one, by twos and by threes, and finally by the hundreds, men in gray began ebbing back down the slope of Cemetery Ridge. Federal officers tried fruitlessly to get their shaken troops to pursue the withdrawing enemy; attempting to lead his

19th Maine beyond the wall, General Gibbon was shot through the shoulder and had to be led from the field.

Farther south, Hancock too was grievously wounded. A Minié ball tore through the pommel of Hancock's saddle and into his thigh, carrying with it several splinters and a bent tenpenny nail. Lowered to the ground by two of Stannard's staff officers, Hancock extracted the nail, which he evidently thought had been fired at him by the enemy. "They must be hard up for ammunition," he gasped, "when they throw such shot as that." Only the application of a tourniquet saved Hancock's life; a little later, he was carried away on a stretcher.

General Pickett had watched it all from the Codori farm just east of the Emmitsburg road. With all his aides away on errands, he was alone as his men came trudging back from the little clump of trees. After a final, forlorn attempt by Trimble's division to break Hays's line to the north — an attack which cost Trimble his left leg — Pickett wheeled his horse and rode away. Later, meeting Lee, he was instructed to prepare his division to repel a possible counterattack. "General Lee," said Pickett, "I have no division now." Pickett's words were close to the truth. He had lost nearly 3,000 men — or more than half of his complement — in the charge, and the division's officer corps had been virtually annihilated. Every one of the 15 regimental commanders had fallen, as had 16 of 17 field officers under them. Two brigadier generals and six colonels were among the division's dead.

For the rest of his life, Pickett would grieve for his men lost that day and would blame Lee for the disaster. Thus, five years after the War, when Pickett and the Confederate guerrilla leader John Mosby paid a courtesy call on Lee in Richmond, the atmosphere was less than cordial. On departing, Pickett launched into a bitter diatribe. "That old man," he said, "had my division slaughtered at Gettysburg."

For an instant of memory, men in gray marched beneath fluttering flags up a long, grassy slope. Then Mosby broke the silence. "Well," he said, "it made you immortal."

While Pickett's shattered units were still straggling back to Seminary Ridge in the lengthening shadows of late afternoon, Alfred Pleasonton, the cocky cavalry chief of the Army of the Potomac, rode up to General

Meade. "I will give you half an hour to show yourself a great general," Pleasonton declared. "Order the army to advance, while I take the cavalry and get in Lee's rear, and we will finish the campaign in a week."

For once restraining his notorious temper at this gratuitous advice from a subordinate, Meade answered mildly: "How do you know Lee will not attack me again?" Complacently, he added, "We have done well enough."

In command of the army for only six days, Meade had spent three of them fighting one of history's most ferocious battles, and he had held his ground. To move now from the

Struck by five bullets, Brigadier General Elon J. Farnsworth falls dead from his horse as his cavalry brigade charges Longstreet's right wing near Big Round Top. The foolhardy attack, ordered by General Judson Kilpatrick over Farnsworth's strenuous objections, failed dismally and ended the third day's fighting at Gettysburg.

confirmed. Patrols reported that Lee had pulled back his left wing, clearing Gettysburg and the areas to the north and east, and that Longstreet was gone from the Peach Orchard salient. Yet when Federal skirmishers advanced to the Emmitsburg road, they came under brisk fire from the woods on Seminary Ridge. Lee was still there, apparently inviting attack, just as he had done — with dire consequences to the Army of the Potomac — at Second Bull Run, Antietam and Fredericksburg.

Moreover, Meade had the condition of his own army to consider. An early-morning head count on July 4 showed only 51,414 officers and men reporting for duty. This seemed to indicate that more than 38,000 men had been lost in the battle. In fact, almost 15,000 of those merely had been separated from their outfits during the fighting and would soon return. But Meade could hardly be expected to know that.

Most of the losses — 23,049 by actual count — had been suffered by four of Meade's seven corps; in fact, two of them, I and III Corps, would eventually pass from existence, the men being dispersed to other commands. Any assault, then, would have to rely on three corps attacking a Confederate army that, however badly hurt, had never in the War been dislodged from a defensive position. The prospect was daunting — and Meade decided against it.

Thus, while the opposing armies glowered at each other from ridges scarcely a mile apart, Meade contented himself with occupying Gettysburg and sending out patrols and burial parties. Men with time to spare walked out on the field of battle. One of them was Sergeant Thomas Marbaker of the 11th New Jersey, who later recorded his

defensive to the offensive would be a task of awesome difficulty, especially with that long line of Confederate cannon still glaring at him from the west. As General Hunt later elaborated, "A prompt counter-charge after combat between two small bodies of men is one thing; the change from the defensive to the offensive of an army is quite another. To have made such a change to the offensive, on the assumption that Lee had made no provision against a reverse, would have been rash in the extreme."

Meade was anything but rash, and the next day, July 4, his judgment seemed to be

impressions of the unforgettable scene:

"Upon the open fields, like sheaves bound by the reaper, in crevices of the rocks, behind fences, trees and buildings; in thickets, where they had crept for safety only to die in agony; by stream or wall or hedge, wherever the battle had raged or their weakening steps could carry them, lay the dead. Some, with faces bloated and blackened beyond recognition, lay with glassy eyes staring up at the blazing summer sun; others, with faces downward and clenched hands filled with grass or earth, which told of the agony of the last moments.

"Here a headless trunk, there a severed limb; in all the grotesque positions that unbearable pain and intense suffering contorts the human form, they lay. Upon the faces of some death had frozen a smile; some showed the trembling shadow of fear, while upon others was indelibly set the grim stamp of determination.

"All around was the wreck the battlestorm leaves in its wake — broken caissons, dismounted guns, small arms bent and twisted by the storm or dropped and scattered by disabled hands; dead and bloated horses, torn and ragged equipments, and all the sorrowful wreck that the waves of battle leave at their ebb; and over all, hugging the earth like a fog, poisoning every breath, the pestilential stench of decaying humanity."

At about 1 p.m. on July 4, sullen clouds rolled across the region, thunder roared, lightning cracked, and there began a deluge that, as one man put it, "washed the blood from the grass."

Against that apocalyptic backdrop, General Meade composed his congratulations to the Army of the Potomac, concluding with an exhortation he would later regret: "Our task is not yet accomplished, and the commanding general looks to the army for greater efforts to drive from our soil every vestige of the presence of the invader."

Since the beginning of the War, Abraham Lincoln had been trying to convince his successive commanders that their objective should be not the possession of real estate but the destruction of Lee's army. Thus, upon reading Meade's message, Lincoln's face darkened; he slapped his knee in frustration and groaned: "Drive the invader from our soil? My God! Is that all?"

Robert E. Lee, meanwhile, knew what he must do. His casualties were too high, his ammunition and supplies too low to remain in enemy territory. As he told one subordinate after the sound of the guns had faded: "We must now return to Virginia."

But getting there was another matter, and it would call forth all of Lee's capacities for active leadership. Late into the night of July 3 he labored, studying maps in the flickering candlelight of his tent and issuing a stream of orders.

Among the first to get instructions was Brigadier General John Imboden, whose cavalry brigade had not arrived at Gettysburg until noon on July 3. Summoned that night to army headquarters, Imboden had to wait until 1 a.m. for Lee's return. Then, Imboden recalled, "He came riding alone, at a slow walk, and evidently wrapped in profound thought." When Lee attempted to dismount, he seemed so exhausted that Imboden stepped forward to assist his chief. But Lee waved him aside and stood leaning against Traveller, supporting himself with his arm across the saddle.

"The moon shone full upon his massive

features," Imboden wrote, "and revealed an expression of sadness I had never seen before upon his face." Embarrassed, Imboden broke the awkward silence. "General," he said, "this has been a hard day for you."

"Yes," replied Lee, "it has been a sad, sad day to us." And then, after a pause of more than a minute, he sighed with infinite regret: "Too bad. Oh! Too bad!"

Recovering himself, Lee gave Imboden a dangerous task — to escort the Confederate wounded and most of the army's supply wagons back to Virginia. First he was to head northwest across South Mountain to Cham-

bersburg, then turn south to Hagerstown and thence to Williamsport on the Potomac, where both a ford and a pontoon bridge awaited him. Imboden would have about 2,100 troopers and 23 guns. Fitzhugh Lee's cavalry brigade and part of Wade Hampton's would guard his rear and flanks.

Until the vulnerable wagon train had cleared the Gettysburg area, Lee's infantry would have to hold Seminary Ridge against any attack. Many of the men were still eager. Asked what the troops would do if the Federals attacked, one soldier had a ready answer: "We will fight them until hell freezes over,

Realizing that the battle is lost, Robert E. Lee rides to the rear among Pickett's shattered forces. "He spoke to nearly every man who passed," Colonel E. Porter Alexander recalled, "using expressions such as: 'Don't be discouraged.' 'It was my fault this time.'"

Mementos from the Battlefield

While fighting still raged near his family's Gettysburg farmhouse, a young school-teacher and writer named J. Howard Wert began to gather up what he called "the thickly littered debris of battle." In the days following the battle, Wert, who had served the Union at Gettysburg as a civilian scout, returned often to the ravaged fields, selecting and carefully identifying items from the debris with a keen eye for the memorable and the poignant: the uniform insignia of a heroic Union officer, a Confederate soldier's picture of a loved one. Wert later joined the Army and was wounded at Petersburg. Throughout the remainder of the War, he continued to collect battlefield objects; a portion of his Gettysburg collection is shown on these pages.

J. Howard Wert as a lieutenant of
the 209th Pennsylvania

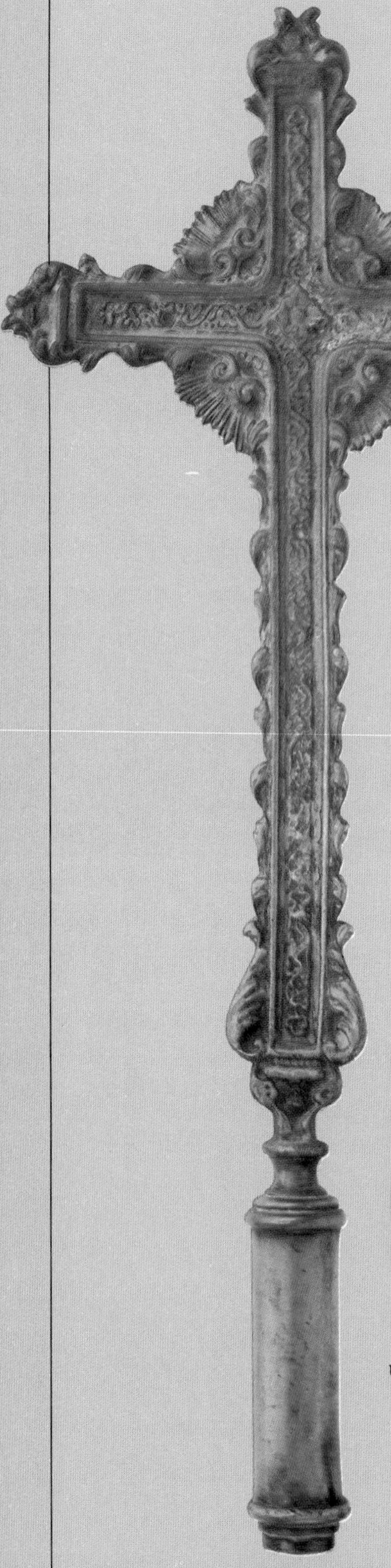

UNION SOLDIER'S COIN PURSE

SHOULDER STRAP OF UNION
COLONEL STRONG VINCENT

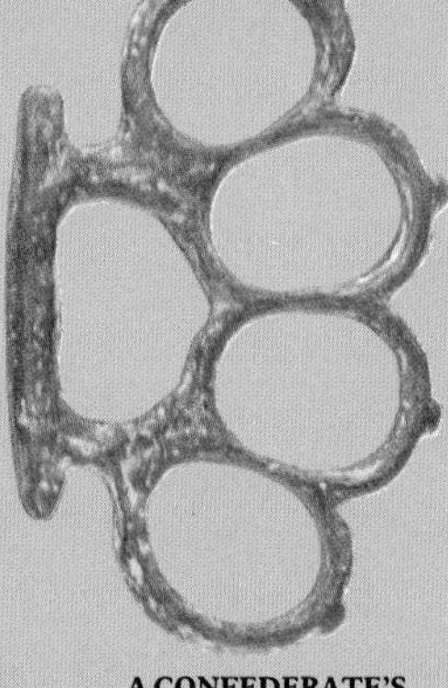

A CONFEDERATE'S
LEAD KNUCKLES

FLAGSTAFF ORNAMENT
OF THE IRISH BRIGADE

LEATHER BLACKJACK CARRIED BY A LOUISIANA TIGER

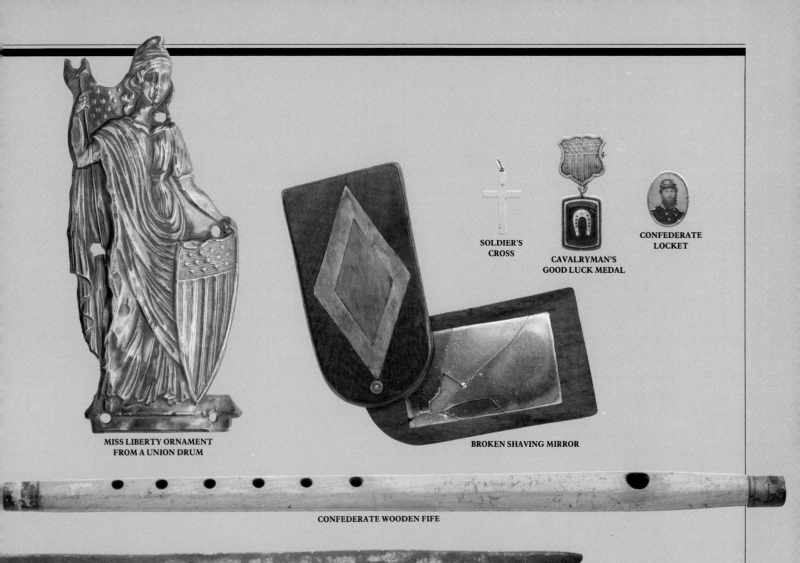

MISS LIBERTY ORNAMENT
FROM A UNION DRUM

BROKEN SHAVING MIRROR

SOLDIER'S
CROSS

CAVALRYMAN'S
GOOD LUCK MEDAL

CONFEDERATE
LOCKET

CONFEDERATE WOODEN FIFE

D-GUARD BOWIE KNIFE

CLOTHING STENCIL OF G. D. WHITNEY

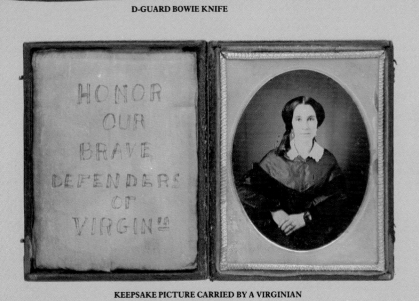

KEEPSAKE PICTURE CARRIED BY A VIRGINIAN

GENERAL HANCOCK'S SADDLE BLANKET INSIGNIA

and then we will fight them on the ice."

Others were not so sure. "Our ammunition was so low," E. Porter Alexander said later, "and our diminished force so widely dispersed along the unwisely extended line, that an advance by a single fresh corps could have cut us in two." As musters were taken on the morning of July 4, the degree of the Confederate disaster became more apparent. Official records would place the army's losses at 20,448, but the actual figure was probably closer to 28,000 — or nearly 40 per cent of those engaged, compared with the Federal casualty rate of 25 per cent.

At 4 p.m. Imboden's wagon train departed on its dismal journey. "The rain fell in blinding sheets," Imboden wrote later. "Canvas was no protection against its fury, and the wounded men lying upon the naked boards of the wagon-bodies were drenched. Horses and mules were blinded and maddened by the wind and water."

Throughout that terrible night the 17-mile-long train lumbered on; by dawn the head of the column was nearing Chambersburg. In Greencastle, 30 or 40 ax-wielding citizens hacked out spokes from the wheels of the passing wagons, toppling a dozen vehicles before Imboden's men could stop them. And then the Federal cavalry appeared, having been unleashed by Meade. As Imboden wrote later, the Federals "began to swarm down upon us from the fields and cross-roads, making their attacks in small bodies, striking the column where there were few or no guards." In time, the Confederate cavalry put a halt to these forays, but some of the wagons were lost to the enemy.

For the wounded, the trip was pure agony. As the vehicles jolted onward over the rough, rocky road, Imboden could hear "such cries

and shrieks as these: 'O God! why can't I die?' 'My God! will no one have mercy and kill me?' Occasionally a wagon would be passed from which only low, deep moans could be heard."

At last, late on the afternoon of July 5, Imboden's lead elements reached Williamsport — only to find that the pontoon bridge had been destroyed by a Federal cavalry detachment and that heavy rain had raised the river and made the ford impassable.

Worse, early the next morning Imboden was informed of the approach of Federal cavalry in strength — as it turned out, the 3,000 men of Buford's division. Wearily, Imboden deployed his somewhat smaller force, in-

The battle flag of the 28th North Carolina was among 33 colors captured by Hancock's II Corps in the repulse of Pickett's Charge. The veteran 28th, part of General James H. Lane's brigade, lost 104 of its 346 men in the disastrous attack.

The Picture That Moved a Nation

After the battle at Gettysburg, a burial detail came upon a dead Union soldier whose only identification was an ambrotype of three young children found clasped in his hand.

Word of these "children of the battlefield" spread; efforts to identify the father blossomed into a Union-wide campaign. Thousands of copies of the picture *(right)* were circulated. A $50 prize was offered for the best poem about the incident, and the winning verse was set to music. Its refrain was a prayer: "O Father, guard the soldier's wife / And for his orphans care."

In November 1863 a woman whose soldier husband was listed as missing recognized the picture as one she had sent him before the battle. He was Sergeant Amos Humiston of Company C, 154th New York Infantry.

The story was not quite over. Proceeds from sales of the photographs and sheet music were used to establish the Soldiers' Orphans' Home in Gettysburg in 1866. Humiston's widow became its first matron, and his children were educated there.

cluding about 700 wagoneers commanded by wounded officers, to meet the threat.

Imboden gambled that the attack would come against his right, where the ground seemed more inviting. He ordered the men on his left to fire, then withdraw until they were concealed behind a low hill and march to the right. The ruse worked: The enemy assault came against the area thus reinforced, and the Confederates held it off until, as night fell, Fitzhugh Lee approached with about 3,000 troopers from the northeast. At the same time, another Confederate cavalry force, led by Jeb Stuart, came down a road farther to the east. The Federal troopers, with their right and rear menaced, broke off their attack and withdrew to the southeast.

Safe for the moment, Imboden settled down to wait for Lee's infantry, which had begun its march immediately after the wagons departed. Rather than following Imboden's easier, roundabout route, the foot soldiers marched on a shorter path to Ha-

gerstown through the rugged high gaps and passes of South Mountain.

Ewell's corps, bringing up the rear, was constantly harassed by enemy cavalry. At Monterey Pass a wildly confused little fight flared in darkness illuminated only by bolts of lightning; Ewell lost many of his wagons, but the strategic results were negligible.

On the morning of July 7, Longstreet's corps led the army into Williamsport. The Potomac was still too high to be crossed on foot, but Imboden had found a couple of small flatboats that could carry about 30 wounded men at a time to the other side. Each trip would take a quarter hour, and moving the more than 10,000 wounded men would require at least 40 hours, even in the unlikely event that nothing went wrong. Still, with no alternative, the task began.

Lee, meanwhile, set his rough-and-ready quartermaster, Major John A. Harman, to work on a new pontoon bridge and ordered his engineers to lay out a defensive line. The

army redeployed, facing generally eastward in an arc along the north-south stretch of the river at Williamsport; Lee's left was anchored at the mouth of Conococheague Creek, just north of the town, and his right near Falling Waters, six miles south. Digging furiously, the Confederates soon built a formidable parapet, six feet wide at the top, with abundant gun emplacements. By the time they were done, many men were actually looking forward to the arrival of the Army of the Potomac. One soldier wrote, "We hope soon to get up another fight."

But General Meade was in no hurry to comply. Not until midday on July 5 did he begin to move his troops out of Gettysburg. Even then, Meade sent only Sedgwick's VI Corps to follow Lee's infantry. At 8:30 the following morning, Sedgwick reported, mistakenly, that Monterey Pass was strongly defended and that he would not

care "to dash my corps against it."

That prospect did not please Meade either. Instead of continuing in Lee's path, he sent his army south along three separate routes into Maryland, then westward across the Catoctin Mountains to a rendezvous at Middletown, where they would still have to cross South Mountain to get at Lee's forces.

On the afternoon of July 6, still at Gettysburg, Meade wired the War Department, complaining about the difficulty of closing with Lee's army. The message sounded timid to President Lincoln, who that night wrote an annoyed note to Halleck. The President said that Meade's actions seemed calculated "to get the enemy across the river again without a further collision, and they do not appear connected with a purpose to prevent his crossing and to destroy him."

The next day—the fourth after the battle—Meade arrived at Frederick, 35 miles south of Gettysburg, where he established

Confederate artillerymen stand by their guns in a section of the nine-mile-long line of earthworks erected between Hagerstown and the Potomac River. The entrenchments, built to cover Lee's retreat, were described by a Federal officer as "the strongest I have seen yet, built as if they meant to stand a month's siege."

his headquarters in the United States Hotel. There he enjoyed a hot bath and, in a letter to his wife, offered what may have been an explanation for the dreamlike pace of his movements. "From the time I took command till today, now over ten days," he wrote, "I have not changed my clothes, have not had a regular night's rest and many nights not a wink of sleep, and for several days did not even wash my face and hands, no regular food, and all the time in a great state of mental anxiety."

In short, Meade was exhausted. His condition was not improved by a flurry of admonitory messages from General Halleck, who was himself being goaded by Lincoln.

"Push forward," Halleck urged, "and fight Lee before he can cross the Potomac." And, later, Halleck wrote: "The President is urgent and anxious that your army should move against Lee by forced marches."

To this, Meade sent an edgy reply. "My army is and has been making forced marches," he wrote, adding on the basis of scattered reports from the field that the troops were "short of rations and barefooted." In fact, supplies had been forwarded in such huge quantities that surpluses had accumulated, and some were already being shipped back to Washington.

By July 9, a large part of Meade's army

Three captive Confederates stand beside a breastwork atop Seminary Ridge, shortly before going off to a prison camp. They were among 5,425 unwounded soldiers captured by Meade's army; another 6,802 wounded fell into Federal hands.

The Terrible Price That Was Paid

The men shown on these pages were among the 50,000 casualties at Gettysburg — 30 per cent of all those engaged — making it the bloodiest single battle fought on American soil. Some, like Colonel Paul Revere, were scions of prominent families. Another man, Private Wesley Culp, was remarkable for the irony of his fate: Culp was killed on his father's farm, fighting for the Confederacy. Many soldiers exhibited a grim fatalism, realizing that they were waging a crucial campaign. Lieutenant Colonel Charles Mudge, ordered to launch a suicidal attack, said simply, "It is murder, but it is the order." He died leading the charge.

PRIVATE DENTON L. THOMPSON
148th Pennsylvania, U.S.A.
Killed

MAJOR BENJAMIN W. LEIGH
1st Virginia Battalion, C.S.A.
Killed

CAPTAIN WILLIAM H. MURRAY
1st Maryland Battalion, C.S.A.
Killed

COLONEL GEORGE L. WILLARD
125th New York, U.S.A.
Killed

PRIVATE JAMES B. LOUGHBRIDGE
Parker's Virginia Battery, C.S.A.
Killed

LIEUT. COL. CHARLES MUDGE
2nd Massachusetts, U.S.A.
Killed

PRIVATE CHARLES A. KEELER
6th Wisconsin, U.S.A.
Wounded

CAPTAIN HERBERT C. MASON
20th Massachusetts, U.S.A.
Wounded

PRIVATES H. J. AND L. J. WALKER
13th North Carolina, C.S.A.
Wounded

LIEUTENANT J. KENT EWING
4th Virginia, C.S.A.
Mortally wounded

MAJOR EDMUND RICE
19th Massachusetts, U.S.A.
Wounded

SERGEANT ROLAND HUDSON
59th Georgia, C.S.A.
Killed

PRIVATE FREDERICK E. WRIGHT
14th Brooklyn, U.S.A.
Killed

LIEUTENANT DANIEL BANTA
66th New York, U.S.A.
Wounded

SERGEANT A. H. COMPTON
8th Virginia, C.S.A.
Wounded and captured

CORPORAL NELSON GILBERT
149th New York, U.S.A.
Wounded

PRIVATE WESLEY CULP
2nd Virginia, C.S.A.
Killed

CAPTAIN LUTHER MARTIN
11th New Jersey, U.S.A.
Killed

SERGEANT FRANCIS STRICKLAND
154th New York, U.S.A.

PRIVATE JOHN HAYDEN
1st Maryland Battalion, C.S.A.

PRIVATE SAMUEL ROYER
149th Pennsylvania, U.S.A.

COLONEL PAUL J. REVERE
20th Massachusetts, U.S.A.

had crossed South Mountain to Boonsboro, eight miles southeast of Williamsport. Meade reported to Halleck, "I think the decisive battle of the war will be fought in a few days." Yet he was still taking no chances: "I desire to adopt such measures as in my judgement will tend to insure success, even though these may be deemed tardy."

The army crept forward, and it was the afternoon of the 12th before Meade announced in a message to Halleck, "It is my intention to attack them tomorrow unless something intervenes to prevent it." Something did intervene: A council of war called by Meade at which he asked his corps commanders to vote on his plan of attack. Two approved, but the other five voted against it, and at 5 p.m. on July 13 Meade informed Washington of the council's results. The attack was off, but he promised to continue with his reconnaissances.

The reaction was a furious message from Halleck: "Act upon your own judgement and make your generals execute your orders. Call no council of war. It is proverbial that councils of war never fight. Do not let the enemy escape." But by then it was too late. The escape was under way.

By the morning of July 13, General Lee's quartermaster had torn down some warehouses for wood, built some makeshift boats and strung across the Potomac at Falling Waters what Colonel Moxley Sorrel described as a "crazy affair." But Lee pronounced it a "good bridge" and ordered the corps of Longstreet and A. P. Hill to start across the river at nightfall. To speed the process, Ewell's corps would use the ford at Williamsport, where the river had at last subsided sufficiently to permit passage.

That afternoon, however, disaster threatened. Heavy rain began to fall, the river started to rise again and the rough dirt road between Williamsport and Falling Waters quickly became a quagmire. Nonetheless, in the pitch-black, eerie night, the movement began. Ewell's men, General Rodes wrote later, had to scramble "down the steep bank of soft and slippery mud. The water was cold, deep and rising. Some small men had to be carried over by their comrades; the water was up to the armpits of a full-sized man."

On the way to Falling Waters, wagons became mired up to their hubs, and the infantrymen were in misery. "The men had to keep their hands on the backs of their file leaders to tell when to move and when to halt," recalled one soldier. "The night being so dark and rainy, we could not see farther than 'the noses on our faces,' while at every step we went nearly up to our knees in slush and mud."

As a dismal dawn approached, Lee received word that nearly all of Ewell's corps had reached the sodden soil of Virginia. But at Falling Waters, where Lee was keeping an anxious watch, Longstreet's corps had just started across the pontoon bridge, while Hill's was still some distance away. A Federal attack now could destroy the Army of Northern Virginia.

Yet even though Federal cavalry had discovered as early as 3 a.m. on the 14th of July that the Confederates were on the move, no attack came. Longstreet's corps crossed the river, followed by most of Hill's. Heth's division, bringing up the rear, was approaching the bridge shortly after 11 a.m., when firing erupted close by. Buford's and Kilpatrick's Federal cavalry were now hot on Lee's trail. "There!" Lee exclaimed, "I was ex-

Troops of the Federal I Corps cross the Potomac on July 18 in belated pursuit of Lee's retreating army. The corps had crossed at the same point the year before, following Lee southward after the Battle of Antietam.

pecting it — the beginning of the attack!"

The most determined assault was led by a regiment in Custer's brigade — the 6th Michigan Cavalry, under Major Peter Weber, who charged General Heth's division. Within three or four minutes, many of the Michigan troopers, including Weber, lay dead. Soon more Federals entered the fray, driving the Confederates back toward the river. In the process, General Pettigrew, commander of Heth's rear guard and one of Lee's most promising officers, was mortally wounded, and nearly 1,500 grayclad infantrymen were taken prisoner. But the defenders had bought time for Lee's escape.

Before long, Lee was watching the last of his troops cross the Potomac. "As the bulk of the rearguard of the army safely passed over the shaky bridge," one Confederate wrote, "as it swayed to and fro, lashed by the current, Lee uttered a sigh of relief, and a great weight seemed taken from his shoulders." As Buford's pursuing horsemen started down the bluff to the river, Lee ordered the bridge cut loose.

In Washington, President Lincoln could not contain his despair. "We had them within our grasp," he told his secretary, John Hay. "We had only to stretch forth our hands and they were ours. And nothing I could say or do could make the army move." Lee had escaped to fight again.

Images of the Aftermath

Two photographs taken and joined by Brady's team (Brady stands at right) offer a panorama of McPherson's Farm and Woods, scene of the battle's first major clash

News that a huge battle had been fought at Gettysburg brought the North's most talented war photographers rushing to the scene. First to arrive were Alexander Gardner and his assistants, Timothy O'Sullivan and James Gibson. Driving their two horse-drawn darkrooms 77 miles to the battlefield from Gardner's Washington studio, the three men began taking pictures on July 5, only two days after the repulse of Pickett's Charge ended the fighting and before many of the dead had been buried. Gardner's aim was to record the horrors of war — and he succeeded.

Next on the scene was the celebrated Mathew Brady. With his own mobile darkrooms and three staff photographers from his New York studio, Brady reached Gettysburg about July 15. By then the dead had been interred, so Brady concentrated on panoramic views of such already-famous fields of combat as Cemetery Hill and Little Round Top. Between them, the Gardner and Brady teams left an indelible record of the landscape where 160,000 Americans struggled for three days and where more than 50,000 of them were killed or wounded.

The Union's hard-fighting Iron Brigade stormed into the woods to repulse Heth's advancing men. The Pennsylvania Bucktails deployed in the field by the pond.

The Lutheran Seminary crowns Seminary Ridge in a Brady photograph. Seized by the Confederates on July 1, the ridge served as a staging area for later assaults.

Two Federal soldiers lounge on the crest of Cemetery Hill about two weeks after the battle, in a panorama attributed to Brady's photographers. On the battle's secon

In a picture by O'Sullivan, Evergreen Cemetery's ornate gate, its windows shot out, looms behind the earthworks of Battery B, 4th U.S. Artillery.

day, the Louisiana Tigers swept up the slope where the two men sit, advancing from the area between Gettysburg *(background)* and Culp's Farm *(far right)*.

One of Brady's assistants gazes
northward toward Cemetery Ridge
from the jumbled Union breastworks
near the crest of Little Round Top.
On July 2, Federal brigades led by
Colonel Strong Vincent and General
Stephen Weed beat off repeated attacks on the stony knob by Alabama
and Texas regiments.

An O'Sullivan photograph taken
on July 6 shows the nightmare landscape of rocks and scraggly trees
called the Slaughter Pen. Burial
details had not reached this rugged area between Big and Little
Round Tops when the picture was
made, and many bodies can be dis-
cerned lying amid the tangle.

A young Confederate soldier lies dead in a sharpshooter's nest in the Devil's Den. Evidence suggests that the photographer — probably O'Sullivan — had the body moved about 40 yards for dramatic effect. The soldier most likely died during a charge toward Little Round Top.

Confederate dead are sprawled near the rock-choked bank of Plum Run, a small stream running through the Slaughter Pen. After brutal hand-to-hand fighting, the 44th Alabama drove Union troops from the area, but the Confederates never succeeded in taking nearby Little Round Top.

Photographed by Alexander Gardner, this Confederate soldier, who was killed by a shell near the Rose Farm, probably belonged to the 51st or 53rd Georgia. Those regiments attacked on July 2 during the prolonged assault by Longstreet's corps against the Federal left.

Shattered stone fences and dead horses show the effect of the two-hour Confederate cannonade that drove General Meade from his headquarters in the Leister farmhouse (center) on July 3. Gardner took the photograph on July 6 from a vantage point on the Taneytown Road.

Union corpses litter a trampled meadow near the Peach Orchard as a burial detail gathers in the distance. The bodies are without shoes, indicating that Confederate troops who held the area on July 2 had scavenged needed gear from the dead. Gardner's caption for this O'Sullivan photograph summed up the terrible nature of the battle: *A Harvest of Death.*

An Address at Gettysburg

Four score and seven years ago our fathers brought forth on this continent, a new nation, conceived in Liberty, and dedicated to the proposition that all men are created equal.

Now we are engaged in a great civil war, testing whether that nation, or any nation so conceived and so dedicated, can long endure. We are met on a great battle field of that war. We have come to dedicate a portion of that field, as a final resting place for those who here gave their lives that that nation might live. It is altogether fitting and proper that we should do this.

But, in a larger sense, we can not dedicate— we can not consecrate— we can not hallow— this ground. The brave men, living and dead, who struggled here, have con-

At the dedication of the Gettysburg National Cemetery, President Lincoln — bareheaded and peering down just to the right of center — prepares to give a brief address.

170

secrated it, far above our poor power to add or detract. The world will little note, nor long remember what we say here, but it can never forget what they did here. It is for us the living, rather, to be dedicated here to the unfinished work which they who fought here have thus far so nobly advanced. It is rather for us to be here dedicated to the great task remaining before us — that

from these honored dead we take increased devotion to that cause for which they gave the last full measure of devotion — that we here highly resolve that these dead shall not have died in vain — that this nation, under God, shall have a new birth of freedom — and that government of the people, by the people, for the people, shall not perish from the earth.

Abraham Lincoln.

November 19, 1863.

Orator Edward Everett, who spoke before Lincoln, later wrote: "I should be glad if I came as near to the central idea in two hours as you did in two minutes."

ACKNOWLEDGMENTS

The editors thank the following individuals and institutions for their valuable assistance in the preparation of this volume:

Alabama: Mobile — Jean Lankford, Jay P. Altmayer Collection.

Connecticut: Hartford — Wilfred Stebbins, The Wadsworth Atheneum. Stamford — Don Troiani. Westport — William Gladstone.

Indiana: South Bend — Stephen Moriarty; Robert Smogor, Snite Museum, University of Notre Dame.

Louisiana: New Orleans — Pat McWhorter, Jan White, The Historic New Orleans Collection.

Maryland: Baltimore — Erick Davis. Clinton — William Turner. Linthicum Heights — Dave Mark. Smithsburg — Thomas Clemens.

Michigan: Dearborn — Donald Baut, Dearborn Historical Museum.

Minnesota: St. Paul — Lyn Anderson; Thomas O'Sullivan, Dona Sieden, Bonnie Wilson, Minnesota Historical Society.

Missouri: Springfield — Dr. Thomas P. Sweeney.

Montana: Crow Agency — James Court, Neil Mangum, Custer Battlefield National Monument.

New York: Albany — Gene Deaton, Camille O'Leary, State of New York, Division of Military and Naval Affairs. Cooperstown — Donna Cornell, National Baseball Hall of Fame Library.

Ohio: Niles — James Frasca.

Pennsylvania: Enola — Caba Craig. Carlisle — Randy Hackenburg, Michael J. Winey, U.S. Army Military History Institute. Gettysburg — Larry Eckert, Kathleen R. Georg, John Heiser, Raymond Morris, James Roach, James Troxell, Gettysburg National Military Park. Gladwyne — Terence P. O'Leary. Harrisburg — William C. Davis, Historical Times, Inc.; Richard A. Sauers, Pennsylvania Capitol Preservation Committee; Bruce Bazelon, Carl R. Nold, Linda Ries, Donald Winer, The State Museum of Pennsylvania. Media — John N. Ockerbloom. Philadelphia — Mr. and Mrs. Manuel Kean, Kean Archives; Russ Pritchard, MOLLUS War Library and Museum. Pittsburgh — Bruno Krsul, Soldier's and Sail-

or's Memorial Hall; Albert Richardson. Upper Darby — Craig Nannos.

Rhode Island: Providence — Major General John W. Kiely.

Tennessee: Nashville — Herb Peck Jr.

Texas: Bryan — John M. Carroll.

Virginia: Falls Church — Chris Nelson. Leesburg — John Divine. Richmond — Edmund M. Archer; Charlene Alling, David Hahn, Museum of the Confederacy; Sara Shields, Valentine Museum.

Washington, D.C.: Larry Claiborne, Dr. Frank Johnson, Armed Forces Medical Museum; Eveline Nave, Photoduplication Service, Library of Congress; Barbara Burger, Deborah Edge and staff, National Archives, Still Pictures Branch.

Wisconsin: Madison — George Talbot, Iconography Collections, State Historical Society of Wisconsin.

The following source was particularly valuable in the preparation of this volume: *Gettysburg: A Journey in Time* by William A. Frassanito, Scribner, 1975.

The index was prepared by Nicholas J. Anthony.

BIBLIOGRAPHY

Books

Alexander, E. P., *Military Memoirs of a Confederate.* Dayton: Morningside Bookshop, 1977 (reprint of 1907 edition).

Bandy, Ken, and Florence Freeland, comps., *The Gettysburg Papers.* 2 vols. Dayton: Morningside Bookshop, 1978.

Banes, Charles H., *History of the Philadelphia Brigade.* Gaithersburg, Md.: Butternut Press, 1984 (reprint of 1876 edition).

Beale, George W., *A Lieutenant of Cavalry in Lee's Army.* Boston: The Gorham Press, 1918.

Bigelow, John, *The Peach Orchard: Gettysburg, July 2, 1863.* Minneapolis: Kimball-Storer, 1910.

Blackford, W. W., *War Years with Jeb Stuart.* New York: Scribner, 1945.

Bond, W. R., *Pickett or Pettigrew?* Gaithersburg, Md.: Butternut Press, 1984 (reprint of 1888 edition).

Buell, Augustus, *The Cannoneer: Recollections of Service in the Army of the Potomac.* Washington: National Tribune, 1890.

Caldwell, J.F.J., *The History of a Brigade of South Carolinians.* Philadelphia: King & Baird, 1866.

Catton, Bruce, *Gettysburg: The Final Fury.* New York: Berkley Books, 1974.

Clark, Walter, ed., *Histories of the Several Regiments and Battalions from North Carolina in the Great War 1861-'65.* Vols. 1-4. Wendell, N.C.: Broadfoot's Bookmark, 1982 (reprint of 1901 edition).

Cleaves, Freeman, *Meade of Gettysburg.* Dayton: Morningside Bookshop, 1980.

Coddington, Edwin B., *The Gettysburg Campaign: A Study in Command.* New York: Scribner, 1968.

Crowninshield, Benjamin W., *A History of the First Regiment of Massachusetts Cavalry Volunteers.* Boston: Houghton, Mifflin, 1891.

Curtis, O. B., *History of the Twenty-fourth Michigan of the Iron Brigade.* Gaithersburg, Md.: Butternut Press, 1984 (reprint of 1891 edition).

Davis, Burke, *Jeb Stuart: The Last Cavalier.* New York: Rinehart, 1957.

Denison, Frederic, *Sabres and Spurs.* The First Rhode Island Cavalry Veteran Association, 1876.

De Trobriand, Régis, *Four Years with the Army of the Potomac.* Transl. by George K. Dauchy. Boston: Ticknor, 1889.

Dickert, D. Augustus, *History of Kershaw's Brigade.* Dayton:

Morningside Bookshop, 1976 (reprint of 1899 edition).

Divine, John J., *8th Virginia Infantry.* Lynchburg, Va.: H. E. Howard, 1983.

Downey, Fairfax, *Clash of Cavalry: The Battle of Brandy Station.* New York: David McKay Company, 1959.

Dunkelman, Mark H., and Michael J. Winey, *The Hardtack Regiment: An Illustrated History of the 154th Regiment, New York State Infantry Volunteers.* East Brunswick, N.J.: Associated University Presses, 1981.

Frassanito, William A., *Gettysburg: A Journey in Time.* New York: Scribner, 1975.

Freeman, Douglas Southall, *Lee's Lieutenants: A Study in Command.* Vol. 3. New York: Scribner, 1944.

Frost, Lawrence A., *The Custer Album.* Seattle: Superior Publishings, 1964.

Gibbon, John, *Personal Recollections of the Civil War.* Dayton: Morningside Bookshop, 1978 (reprint of 1928 edition).

Goldsborough, W. W., *The Maryland Line in the Confederate Army: 1861-1865.* Gaithersburg, Md.: Butternut Press, 1983 (reprint of 1900 edition).

Gordon, John B., *Reminiscences of the Civil War.* New York: Scribner, 1903.

Goss, Warren Lee, *Recollections of a Private: A Story of the Army of the Potomac.* New York: Thomas Y. Crowell, 1890.

Gracey, S. L., *Annals of the Sixth Pennsylvania Cavalry.* E. H. Butler, 1868.

Harrison, Walter, *Pickett's Men.* Gaithersburg, Md.: Butternut Press, 1984 (reprint of 1870 edition).

Haskel, Frank Aretas, *The Battle of Gettysburg.* Wisconsin History Commission, 1908.

Hassler, Warren W., Jr., *Crisis at the Crossroads.* University, Ala.: University of Alabama Press, 1970.

Heth, Henry, *The Memoirs of Henry Heth.* Ed. by James L. Morrison Jr. Westport, Conn.: Greenwood Press, 1974.

Hoke, Jacob, *The Great Invasion.* New York: Thomas Yoseloff, 1959.

Johnson, Robert Underwood, and Clarence Clough Buel, eds.:

Battles and Leaders of the Civil War. Vol. 3. New York: Century, 1887.

Retreat from Gettysburg. New York: Castle Books, 1956.

Krick, Robert K., *Lee's Colonels.* Dayton: Morningside Bookshop, 1979.

Lloyd, William Penn, *History of the First Reg't Pennsylvania Reserve Cavalry.* Philadelphia: King & Baird, 1864.

Longacre, Edward G., *The Man behind the Guns.* New York: A. S. Barnes, 1977.

Longstreet, James, *From Manassas to Appomattox.* Ed. by James I. Robertson Jr. Bloomington: Indiana University Press, 1960.

McClellan, H. B., *I Rode with Jeb Stuart.* Millwood, N.J.: Kraus Reprint, 1981.

McFeely, William S., *Grant: A Biography.* New York: W. W. Norton, 1981.

McKim, Randolph H., *A Soldier's Recollections.* New York: Longmans, Green, 1910.

Maine Gettysburg Commissioners' Executive Committee, *Maine at Gettysburg.* Portland, Me.: Lakeside Press, 1898.

Meade, George Gordon, *The Life and Letters of George Gordon Meade.* Vol. 2. New York: Scribner, 1913.

Mellon, James, comp. and ed., *The Face of Lincoln.* New York: Viking, 1979.

Neese, George M., *Three Years in the Confederate Horse Artillery.* Dayton: Morningside Bookshop, 1983.

Nevins, Allan, ed., *A Diary of Battle: The Personal Journals of Colonel Charles S. Wainwright, 1861-1865.* New York: Harcourt, Brace & World, 1962.

New York Monuments Commission, *In Memoriam Alexander Stewart Webb 1835-1911.* Albany, N.Y.: J. B. Lyon, 1916.

Norton, Henry, comp. and ed., *Deeds of Daring, or History of the Eighth N.Y. Volunteer Cavalry.* Norwich, N.Y.: Chenango Telegraph Printing House, 1889.

Norton, Oliver Willcox, *The Attack and Defense of Little Round Top.* Dayton: Morningside Bookshop, 1978.

Nye, Wilbur Sturtevant, *Here Come the Rebels!* Baton Rouge: Louisiana State University Press, 1965.

Oates, William C., *The War between the Union and the Confederacy and Its Lost Opportunities.* New York: Neale Publishing, 1905.

Perry, Bliss, *Life and Letters of Henry Lee Higginson.* Boston: The Atlantic Monthly Press, 1921.

Pickerill, W. N., *History of the Third Indiana Cavalry.* Indianapolis: Aetna Printing, 1906.

Pickett, George E., *The Heart of a Soldier.* New York: Seth Moyle, 1913.

Pullen, John J., *The Twentieth Maine.* Dayton: Morningside

Bookshop, 1957.

Pyne, Henry R., *Ride to War: The History of the First New Jersey Cavalry.* Ed. by Earl Schenck Miers. New Brunswick, N.J.: Rutgers University Press, 1961.

Rea, Lilian, ed., *War Record and Personal Experiences of Walter Raleigh Robbins.* Privately printed, 1923.

Regimental History Committee, *History of the Nineteenth Regiment: Massachusetts Volunteer Infantry 1861-1865.* Salem, Mass.: Salem Press, 1906.

Simpson, Harold B., *Hood's Texas Brigade: Lee's Grenadier Guard.* Dallas: Alcor Publishing, 1983.

Smith, James E., *A Famous Battery and Its Campaigns, 1861-'64.* Washington: W. H. Lowdermilk, 1892.

Starr, Stephen Z., *The Union Cavalry in the Civil War.* Vol. 1. Baton Rouge: Louisiana State University Press, 1979.

Stevens, John W., *Reminiscences of the Civil War.* Powhatan, Va.: Derwent Books, 1982 (reprint of 1902 edition).

Stewart, George R., *Pickett's Charge.* Dayton: Morningside Bookshop, 1980.

Stewart, Robert Laird, *History of the One Hundred and Fortieth Regiment Pennsylvania Volunteers.* The Regimental Association, 1912.

Swanberg, W. A., *Sickles the Incredible.* New York: Scribner, 1956.

Thomason, John W., Jr., *Jeb Stuart.* New York: Scribner, 1930.

Tobie, Edward P., *History of the First Maine Cavalry 1861-1865.* Boston: Press of Emery & Huges, 1887.

Tucker, Glenn:
Hancock the Superb. Indianapolis: Bobbs-Merrill, 1960.
High Tide at Gettysburg. Dayton: Morningside Bookshop, 1973.

Lee and Longstreet at Gettysburg. Indianapolis: Bobbs-Merrill, 1968.

United States War Department, *The War of the Rebellion: A Compilation of the Official Records of the Union and Confederate Armies.* Series 1, Vol. 27, Part 2 — Reports. Washington: GPO, 1889.

Van De Water, Frederic F., *Glory-Hunter: A Life of General Custer.* New York: Argosy-Antiquarian, 1963.

Von Borcke, Heros, and Justus Scheibert, *The Great Cavalry Battle of Brandy Station: 9 June 1863.* Transl. by Stuart T. Wright and F. D. Bridgewater. Winston-Salem, N.C.: Palaemon Press, 1976.

Wallace, Willard M., *Soul of the Lion: A Biography of General Joshua L. Chamberlain.* New York: Thomas Nelson & Sons, 1960.

Warner, Ezra J., *Generals in Gray.* Baton Rouge: Louisiana State University Press, 1959.

Weygant, Charles H., *History of the One Hundred and Twenty-fourth Regiment, N.Y.S.V.* Newburgh, N.Y.: Journal Printing House, 1877.

Whittaker, Frederick, *A Popular Life of Gen. George A. Custer.* New York: Sheldon, 1876.

Williams, Kenneth P., *Lincoln Finds a General: A Military Study of the Civil War.* Vol. 2. New York: Macmillan, 1949.

Wise, Jennings Cropper, *The Long Arm of Lee.* New York: Oxford University Press, 1959.

Other Sources

Bixley, Lawrence G., "Bucktails Forward!" *Military Images,* July-August 1980.

Braun, Robert A., "The Fight for Devil's Den: 124th New York vs. Texas Infantry." *Military Images,* July-

August 1983.

Civil War Times Illustrated, Special Gettysburg Edition, July 1963.

Dunkelman, Mark, and Michael J. Winey, "The Hunt for Sergeant Humiston." *Civil War Times Illustrated,* March 1982.

Forbes, Edwin, "As a Battlefield Artist Saw Gettysburg." *Civil War Times Illustrated,* December 1967.

Georg, Kathleen R., "Tipton Panorama Photos of Gettysburg." *Military Images,* September-October 1984.

Gladstone, William, "The Children of the Battlefield." *Military Images,* March-April 1981.

Guelzo, Allen C., "The Fighting Philadelphia Brigade." *Civil War Times Illustrated,* January 1980.

Longacre, Edward:
"John F. Reynolds, General." *Civil War Times Illustrated,* August 1972.
"Target: Winchester, Virginia." *Civil War Times Illustrated,* June 1976.

Magner, Blake A., "The Great Pivot." *Military Images,* November-December 1984.

Nielson, Jon M., "Brandy Station: 'The Prettiest Cavalry Fight.' " *Civil War Times Illustrated,* July 1978.

Sword, Wiley, "Facing the Gray Wave." *Civil War Times Illustrated,* January 1981.

Thompson, Benjamin W., "This Hell of Destruction: The Benjamin W. Thompson Memoir — Part 2." *Civil War Times Illustrated,* October 1973.

Wert, J. Howard, "In the Hospitals of Gettysburg." *Harrisburg Telegraph,* July-September 1907.

Wilson, Clyde N., Jr., "James J. Pettigrew." *Civil War Times Illustrated,* February 1973.

PICTURE CREDITS

Credits from left to right are separated by semicolons, from top to bottom by dashes.

Cover: Painting by Alfred R. Waud, courtesy R. Gordon Barton, The Sporting Gallery, Inc. 2, 3: Map by Peter McGinn. 8, 9: Painting by Thure de Thulstrup, courtesy Seventh Regiment Fund, Inc., photographed by Al Freni. 11: Painting by Thomas Hicks, War Library and Museum of the Military Order of the Loyal Legion of the United States (MOLLUS), photographed by Larry Sherer. 12, 13: Library of Congress. 14, 15: Courtesy Mark Katz, Americana Image Gallery. 17: Valentine Museum, Richmond, Virginia; from *The Great Cavalry Battle of Brandy Station: 9 June 1863,* by Heros von Borcke and Justus Scheibert, published by Palaemon Press, Winston-Salem, North Carolina, 1976. 18: Valentine Museum, Richmond, Virginia. 19: Wadsworth Atheneum, Hartford, The Ella Gallup Sumner and Mary Catlin Sumner Collection, photographed by Joseph Szaszfai. 20, 21: Courtesy Frank & Marie-T. Wood Print Collections, Alexandria, Virginia. 23: The Western Reserve Historical Society, Cleveland, Ohio. 24: From *A Soldier's Recollections: Leaves from the Diary of a Young Confederate,* by Randolph H. McKim, published by Longmans, Green, New York, 1910. 27: Courtesy Thomas R. Cochran Jr.; courtesy William A. Frassanito — from *A Popular Life of Gen. George A. Custer,* by Frederick Whittaker, published by Sheldon, New York, 1876. 28, 29:

Sketches by Alfred R. Waud, Library of Congress — Library of Congress. 31: Painting by Allen C. Redwood, American Heritage Picture Collection. 32: Map by Walter W. Roberts. 33, 34: Library of Congress. 36, 37: Inserts, War Library and Museum, MOLLUS, photographed by Larry Sherer; Museum of the Confederacy, Richmond, Virginia, photographed by Larry Sherer — U.S. Army Military History Institute (USAMHI), copied by A. Pierce Bounds. 38. Courtesy Chris Nelson; National Archives Neg. No. 111-B-2750 — Custer Battlefield National Monument, Crow Agency, Montana, photographed by Dennis Sanders. 39: Courtesy Bill Turner; Valentine Museum, Richmond, Virginia — Museum of the Confederacy, Richmond, Virginia, photographed by Larry Sherer — Museum of the Confederacy, Richmond, Virginia, photographed by Larry Sherer; War Library and Museum, MOLLUS, photographed by Larry Sherer. 40, 41: Photographs courtesy Bill Turner — courtesy Dr. Thomas P. Sweeney; courtesy J. Craig Nannos, except carbine courtesy John N. Ockerbloom, photographed by Larry Sherer (3). 42: Courtesy J. Craig Nannos, photographed by Larry Sherer. 43: Courtesy James C. Frasca Collection, copied by Andy Cifranic; courtesy J. Craig Nannos, photographed by Larry Sherer. 45: Dearborn Historical Museum. 46: Library of Congress. 47: From *Recollections of a Private: A Story of the Army of the Potomac,* by Warren Lee Goss, published by Thomas Y. Crowell, New York, 1890. 48, 49: From *Recollections of a Private: A Story of the Army of the Potomac,* by Warren Lee Goss, published by Thomas Y. Crowell, New York, 1890 — National Archives Negs. Nos. 111-B-192 / 111-B-17. 51: The J. Howard Wert Gettysburg Collection and Civil War Antiq-

uities, photographed by Larry Sherer — drawing by Alfred R. Waud, Library of Congress; courtesy Mark Katz, Americana Image Gallery. 52: From *Battles and Leaders of the Civil War,* Vol. 3, edited by Robert Underwood Johnson and Clarence Clough Buel, published by Century, New York, 1887. 54: Library of Congress. 55: Painting by James E. Taylor, The Huntington Library, San Marino, California. 56, 57: Painting by James Walker, The J. Howard Wert Gettysburg Collection and Civil War Antiquities, photographed by Larry Sherer. 58: Painting by Alfred R. Waud, The Historic New Orleans Collection, 533 Royal Street, Acc. No. 1977.137.2.7. 59: The J. Howard Wert Gettysburg Collection and Civil War Antiquities, photographed by Larry Sherer. 60: National Archives Neg. No. 111-B-2670. 61: Valentine Museum, Richmond, Virginia. 63: Map by Walter W. Roberts. 64: Library of Congress. 65: Courtesy Rochester Museum & Science Center, Rochester, New York. 66: Painting by W. H. Shelton, courtesy Gettysburg National Military Park, photographed by Larry Sherer. 67: Massachusetts Commandery, Military Order of the Loyal Legion and the U.S. Army Military History Institute (MASS/MOLLUS/USAMHI), copied by A. Pierce Bounds. 69: Courtesy James C. Frasca, photographed by Andy Cifranic. 70: Map by Walter W. Roberts. 71: Courtesy Mark Katz, Americana Image Gallery. 72: From *Battles and Leaders of the Civil War,* Vol. 2, published by Century, New York, 1884. 73: Painting by Charles B. Cox, First Regiment Infantry Museum, Philadelphia, photographed by Larry Sherer. 74: Valentine Museum, Richmond, Virginia. 76: National Archives Neg. No. 111-B-4934. 77: From *The War Between the Union and the Confederacy and Its Lost Opportuni-*

ties, by William C. Oates, published by Neale Publishing, New York, 1905. 78: Map by William L. Hezlep. 79: Library of Congress. 80: Etching by Alfred R. Waud, from *Battles and Leaders of the Civil War*, Vol. 3, edited by Robert Underwood Johnson and Clarence Clough Buel, published by Century, New York, 1887. 81: From *The Gettysburg Campaign: A Study in Command*, by Edwin B. Coddington, published by Scribner, New York, 1968. 82, 83: Painting by Peter F. Rothermel, Collections of the State Museum of Pennsylvania, photographed by Henry Groskinsky. 84, 85: Painting by Edwin Forbes, Library of Congress. 86: Drawing by Alfred R. Waud, American Heritage Picture Collection. 87: Library of Congress, courtesy Brian Pohanka. 88-97: Paintings by Peter F. Rothermel, Collections of the State Museum of Pennsylvania, photographed by Henry Groskinsky. 99: "Marse Robert," painted *en grisaille* by William Ludwell Sheppard, courtesy Edmund Archer, photographed by Larry Sherer. 100: Painting by Paul Wood, The Snite Museum of Art, Notre Dame, Indiana, photographed by Steve Moriarty. 101: MASS/MOLLUS/USAMHI, copied by A. Pierce Bounds. 102, 103: Painting by Edwin Forbes, Library of Congress. 105: Kean Archives, Philadelphia, Pennsylvania — The Armed Forces Medical Museum, Armed Forces Institute of Pathology, Washington, D.C., photographed by Dan Cunningham. 106, 107: Library of Congress. 108: Map by William L. Hezlep. 109: The J. Howard Wert Gettysburg Collection and Civil War Antiquities, photographed by Larry Sherer. 110, 111: Painting by Rufus Zogbaum, courtesy Minnesota Historical Society and the State Capitol Building, photographed by Gary Mortenson. 112, 113: MASS/MOLLUS/USAMHI, copied by A. Pierce Bounds — painting by Edwin Forbes, Library of Congress. 114: Chicago Historical Society Neg. No. ICHi-08049. 115: Sketch by Alfred R. Waud, Library of Congress. 116: Painting by Edwin Forbes, Library of Congress. 118: MASS/MOLLUS/USAMHI, copied by A. Pierce Bounds. 120-125: Circular painting by Paul Philippoteaux, Gettysburg National Military Park, photographed by Henry Groskinsky. 127: Rhode Island State House, photographed by Mark Sexton. 129: Painting by Allen C. Redwood, American Heritage Picture Collection. 130: Map by Walter W. Roberts. 131: Valentine Museum, Richmond, Virginia. 132: Painting by H. C. Bispham, courtesy Soldiers and Sailors Memorial Hall, Pittsburgh, photographed by Herbert K. Barnett. 134: From *Battles and Leaders of the Civil War*, Vol. 3, edited by Robert Underwood Johnson and Clarence Clough Buel, published by Century, New York, 1887. 135: Library of Congress. 136, 137: Painting by Edwin Forbes, Library of Congress. 138: Map by William L. Hezlep. 139: Erick Davis Collection, Baltimore, copied by Jeremy N. P. Ross — The Virginia Historical Society, Richmond, Virginia — Valentine Museum, Richmond, Virginia. 140: National Archives Neg. No. 111-B-2522. 141: Painting by Thomas Nast, Private Collection, photograph courtesy Kennedy Galleries, Inc., New York. 142, 143: Painting by James Walker, courtesy Jay P. Altmayer Collection, photographed by Larry Cantrell. 144, 145: Painting by A. G. Richmond, courtesy Soldiers and Sailors Memorial Hall, Pittsburgh, photographed by Herbert K. Barnett. 147: Kean Archives, Philadelphia, Pennsylvania. 148, 149: The J. Howard Wert Gettysburg Collection and Civil War Antiquities, photographed by Larry Sherer. 150: Museum of the Confederacy, photographed by Larry Sherer. 151: The J. Howard Wert Gettysburg Collection and Civil War Antiquities, copied by Larry Sherer. 152: Painting by Edwin Forbes, Library of Congress. 153: National Archives Gift Collection, Photo Number 200(s)-CC-2288. 154: Gettysburg National Military Park; Museum of the Confederacy, Richmond, Virginia — courtesy Dave Mark Collection, copied by Herb Peck Jr.; War Library and Museum, MOLLUS, copied by Larry Sherer; courtesy Bill Turner; MASS/MOLLUS/USAMHI, copied by A. Pierce Bounds — courtesy Alan T. Nolan; USAMHI, copied by A. Pierce Bounds; from *Histories of the Several Regiments and Battalions from North Carolina in the Great War 1861-'65*, Vol. IV, edited by Walter Clark, published by the State, Nash Brothers, Book and Job Printers, Goldsboro, N.C., 1901; courtesy Herb Peck Jr. 155: Courtesy William Gladstone Collection; Gettysburg National Military Park; State of New York, Division of Military & Naval Affairs, copied by Robert Riccardo; courtesy Michael J. McAfee — from *8th Virginia Infantry*, by John E. Divine, © 1983 by H. E. Howard, Inc., Lynchburg, Virginia; courtesy Michael J. McAfee; Gettysburg National Military Park; courtesy Chris Nelson — Pennsylvania Historical and Museum Commission, Division of Archives and Manuscripts, (MG 218-General Photograph Collection); Erick Davis Collection, Baltimore, copied by Jeremy N. P. Ross; courtesy Terence P. O'Leary; The J. Howard Wert Gettysburg Collection and Civil War Antiquities, copied by Larry Sherer. 157: Painting by David Blythe, National Baseball Hall of Fame and Museum, Inc., Cooperstown, New York, photographed by Frank Rollins. 158, 159: Library of Congress. 160, 161: Library of Congress, except bottom right National Archives Neg. No. 111-B-101. 162, 163: Library of Congress. 164, 165: Library of Congress; Library of Congress courtesy William A. Frassanito. 166, 167: Insert MASS/MOLLUS/USAMHI, copied by A. Pierce Bounds; Library of Congress. 168, 169: Library of Congress. 170, 171: Courtesy James Mellon Collection, handwritten text from *The Face of Lincoln*, compiled and edited by James Mellon © 1979 Viking Penguin Inc., published by Viking, New York.

INDEX